Microsoft Project 2013 Expert

Michelle N. Halsey

ISBN-10: 1-64004-142-7

ISBN-13: 978-1-64004-142-4

Silver City Publications & Training, L.L.C.
P.O. Box 1914
Nampa, ID 83653
https://www.silvercitypublications.com/shop/

Contents

Chapter 1 – Working with the Project Environment, Part 1

This chapter introduces you to the *Project Options* dialog box. You will learn about customizing the user interface and display options first. On the Scheduling tab, you will learn about the calendar and scheduling customization. You can control proofing, saving, and language options as well. Finally, we will take a brief look at the many options on the Advanced tab, where you can control a number of settings for how Project works.

Setting General and Display Options

To open the Project Options dialog box, use the following procedure.

Step 1: Select the **File** tab from the Ribbon to open the Backstage View.

Step 2: Select **Options**.

The *Project Options* dialog box opens to the *General* tab.

- Select an option from the drop down box to select a new **Color scheme**.

- Select an option from the drop down box to indicate how you want to use **ScreenTips**.

- Select a **Default view** from the drop down list.

- Select a **Date format** from the drop down list.

- Enter your **User name** and **Initials** to personalize your copy of Project.

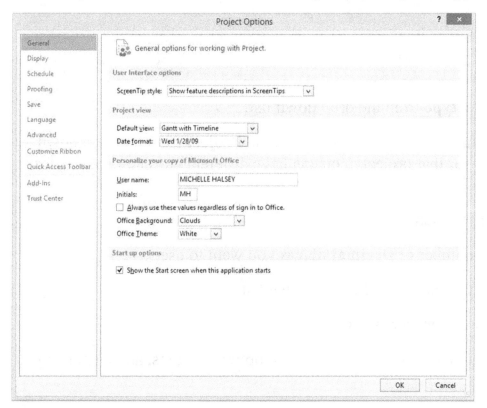

The *Display* tab of the *Project Options* dialog box.

Step 1: Select the **Display** tab from the left.

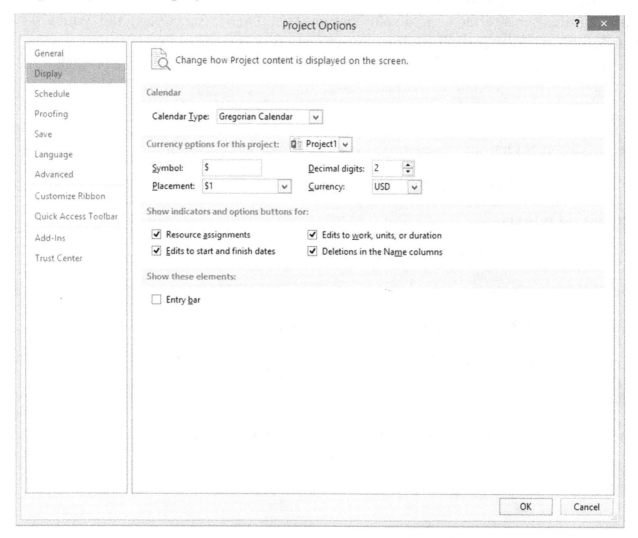

Step 2: Select the **Calendar type** from the drop down list.

Step 3: If you have more than one project open, select the **Project** from the drop down list to set currency options for that project. You can have different currency options for each project.

Step 4: Enter the **Symbol** you want to use.

Step 5: Enter or select the number of **Decimal places** you want to use.

Step 6: Select a **Placement** option from the drop down list.

Step 7: Select a **Currency** option from the drop down list.

Step 8: Check the box(es) to indicate which indicators, options buttons, and elements you want to show.

Setting Calendar and Schedule Options

The *Schedule* tab on the *Project Options* dialog box.

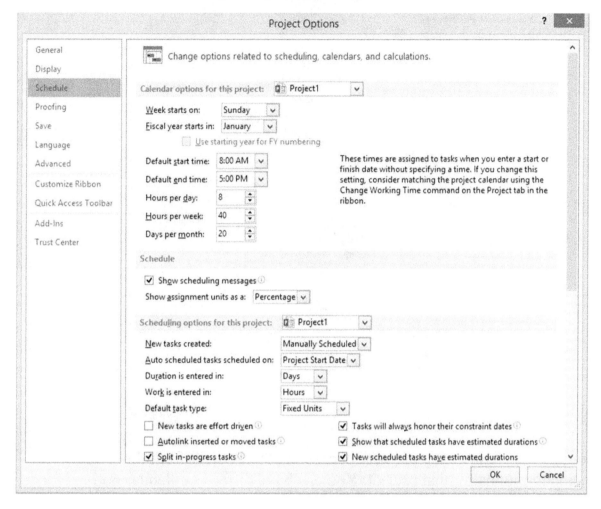

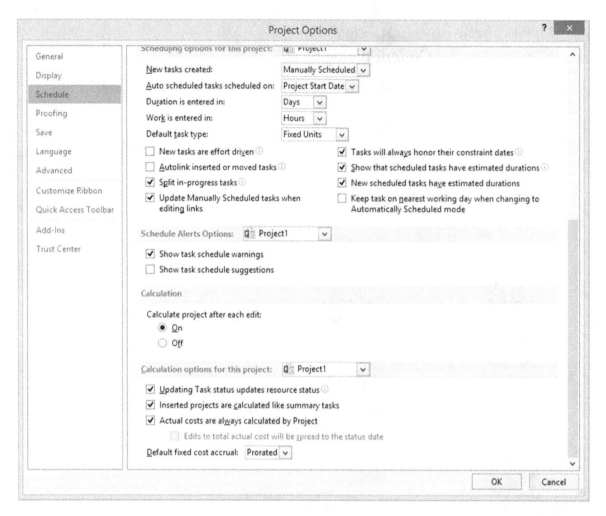

Step 1: If you have more than one project open, select the **Project** from the drop down list to set calendar options for that project. You can have different calendar options for each project.

- Select a **Week Starting Day** from the drop down list.

- Select a **Starting Month** for the fiscal year form the drop down list

- Select a **Default Start** and **End time** from the drop down lists.

- Enter the **Hours per Day**, the **Hours per Week**, and the **Days per Month**.

- Check the box to indicate whether to **Show scheduling messages**.

- Select an option from the **Show Assignment Units** drop down list.

Step 2: If you have more than one project open, select the **Project** from the drop down list to set scheduling options for that project. You can have different scheduling options for each project.

- Select how **New Tasks** are created from the drop down list.

- Indicate how **Auto scheduled tasks** are scheduled from the drop down list.

- Select how **Duration** is entered from the drop down list.

- Select the time unit for **Work** from the drop down list.

- Select a **default task type** from the drop down list.

- Check the box(es) to indicate how the listed items are handled.

Step 3: If you have more than one project open, select the **Project** from the drop down list to set schedule alert options for that project. You can have different schedule alert options for each project.

- Check the box(es) to indicate which warnings and suggestions to show.

Step 4: Indicate whether to Calculate the project after each edit.

Step 5: If you have more than one project open, select the **Project** from the drop down list to set calculation options for that project. You can have different calculation options for each project.

- Check the box(es) to indicate the calculation options.

- Select a Default fixed cost accrual option from the drop down list.

Setting Proofing, Saving, and Language Options

The **Proofing** tab in the *Project Options* dialog box. This tab allows you to control how Project corrects text as you type and how your spelling is corrected.

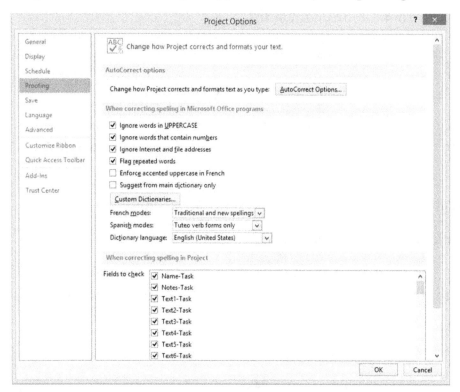

Select the **AutoCorrect Options** button to open the AutoCorrect dialog box.

Select the **Custom Dictionaries** button to open the Custom Dictionaries dialog box.

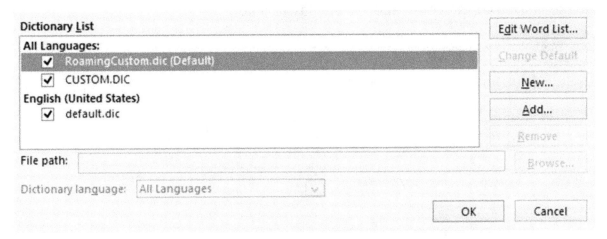

The **Save** tab on the *Project Options* dialog box. This tab allows you to control the format and location of your files when they are saved. You can also indicate a frequency for automatic saves. It also controls your template location and cache size and location.

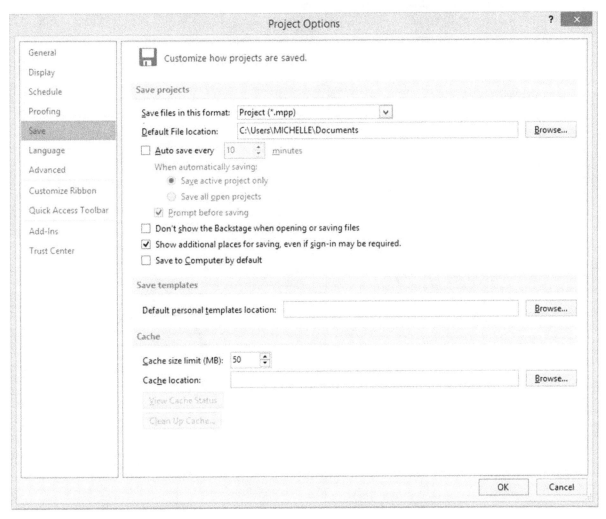

The **Language** tab in the *Project Options* dialog box. This tab allows you to control which language is used for proofing and for display and help.

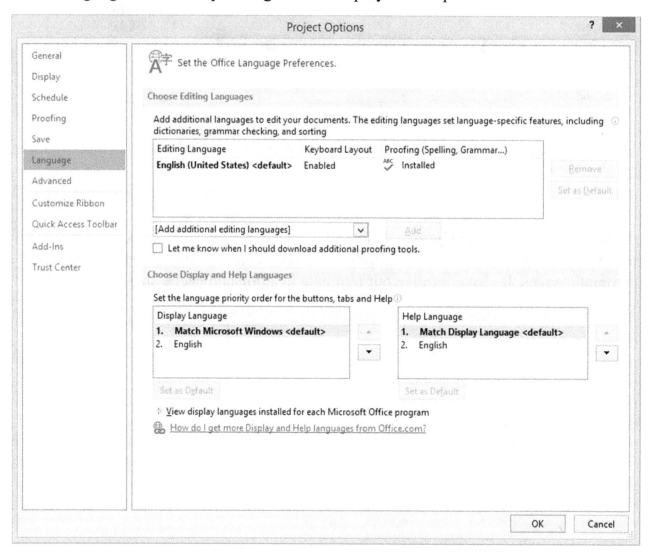

Setting Advanced Options

The *Advanced* tab on the *Project Options* dialog box.

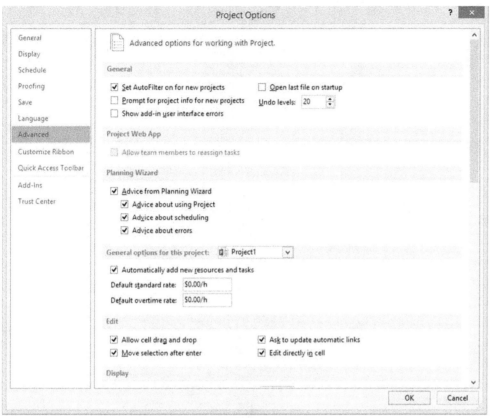

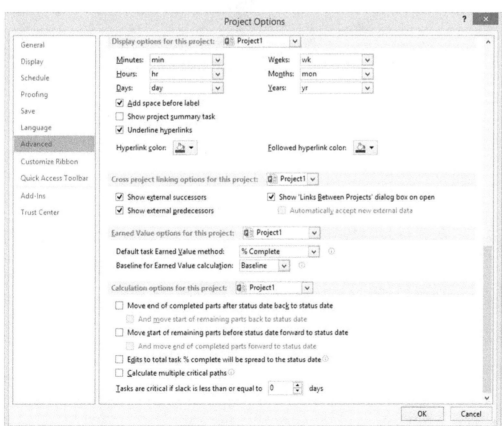

Chapter 2- Working with the Project Environment, Part 2

This chapter addresses a few additional items for customizing your Project environment. You can customize the Ribbon or the Quick Access Toolbar. You will also practice setting some common settings by setting the default task type and the default assignment unit format.

Customizing the Ribbon

To customize the Ribbon, use the following procedure.

Step 1: Select the **File** tab from the Ribbon to open the Backstage View.

Step 2: Select **Options**.

Step 3: Select **Customize Ribbon** from the left side.

In the left column, under Choose Commands From, Project lists the commands available in the application. You can choose a different option from the **Choose Commands From** drop down list to change which options are shown or how they are sorted.

The right column shows the available tabs on the Ribbon.

Step 4: To customize the Ribbon, select the command that you want to change on the left column. Select **Add**. You may need to create a Custom Group before you can add a command.

- Select the Tab where you want the group to appear.

- Select **New Group**.

- Enter the Group name.

You can also remove commands or rearrange them on the right column.

When you have finished, select **OK**.

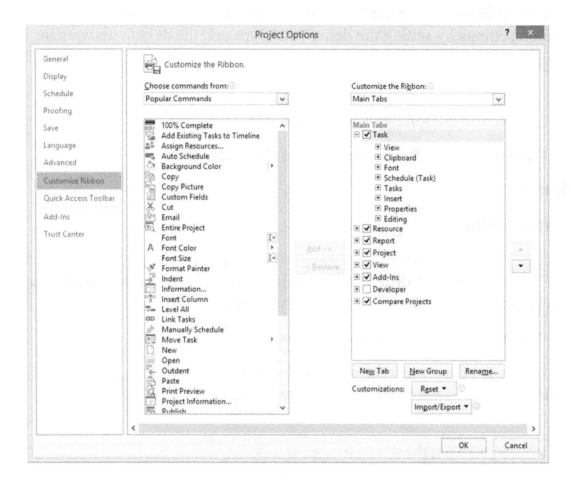

Customizing the Quick Access Toolbar

To customize the Quick Access Toolbar, use the following procedure.

Step 1: Select the **File** tab from the Ribbon to open the Backstage View.

Step 2: Select **Options**.

Step 3: Select **Quick Access Toolbar** from the left side.

In the left column, under **Choose Commands From**, Project lists the commands available in the application. You can choose a different option from the **Choose Commands From** drop down list to change which options are shown or how they are sorted.

The right column shows the available commands on the Quick Access toolbar.

Step 4: To customize the Quick Access toolbar, select the command that you want to change on the left column. Select **Add**.

You can also remove commands or rearrange them on the right column.

When you have finished, select **OK**.

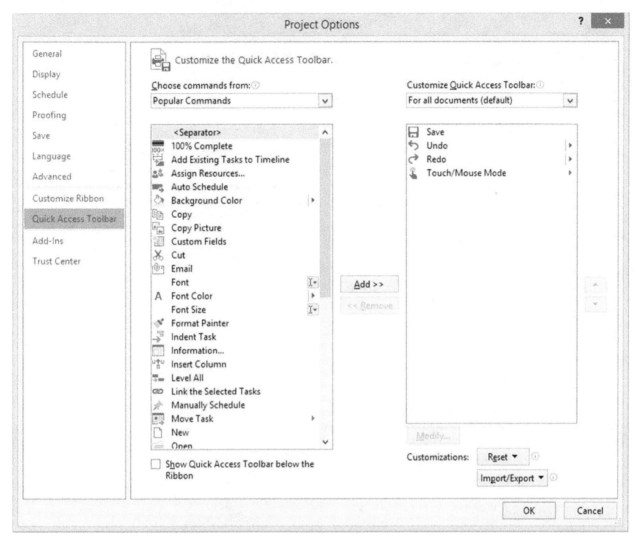

Setting Default Task Types

To set the default task type, use the following procedure.

Step 1: Select the **File** tab from the Ribbon to open the Backstage View.

Step 2: Select **Options**.

Step 3: Select the *Schedule* tab.

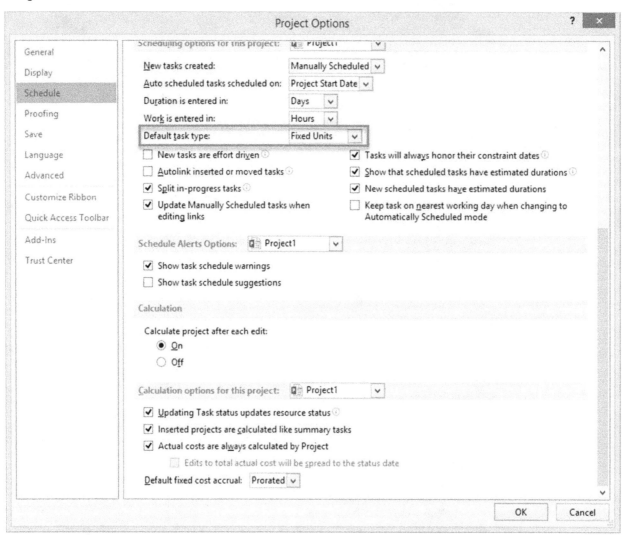

Step 4: Under the Scheduling options header, select the **Default Task Type** from the drop down list. You can choose from Fixed Units, Fixed Duration, or Fixed Work.

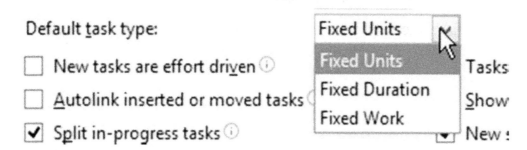

Changing the Default Assignment Unit Format

To set the default assignment unit format, use the following procedure.

Step 1: Select the **File** tab from the Ribbon to open the Backstage View.

Step 2: Select **Options**.

Step 3: Select the *Schedule* tab.

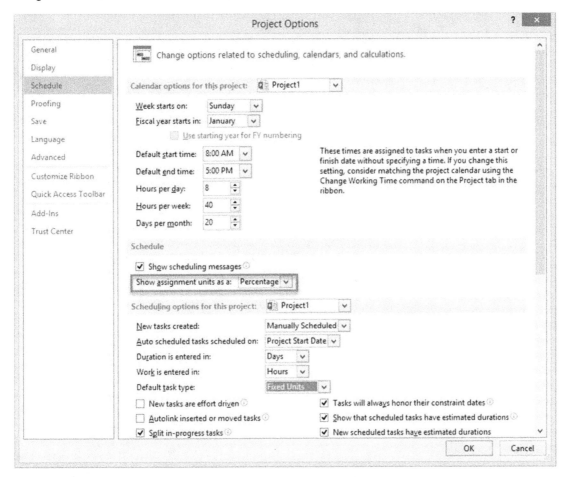

Step 4: Select an assignment unit format from the **Show assignment units as a** drop down list under the Schedule heading. You can select Percentage or Decimal.

Chapter 3 – Templates and Other New Project Time Savers

This chapter will help you get your new projects up and running even faster than before. You will learn how to create templates so that you can capture a completed project and use it repeatedly for future projects. You will also learn how to create a project from an existing project. This chapter also explores Project's capabilities of creating project plans from other file formats. First, we will create a project plan from a SharePoint task list. Finally, we will create a project plan from a Microsoft Excel workbook.

Creating a Template from a Completed Project

To save a completed project as a template, use the following procedure.

Step 1: Select the **File** tab from the Ribbon to open the Backstage view.

Step 2: Select **Save As**.

Step 3: In the *Save As* dialog box, select **Project Template** from the **Save As Type** drop down list.

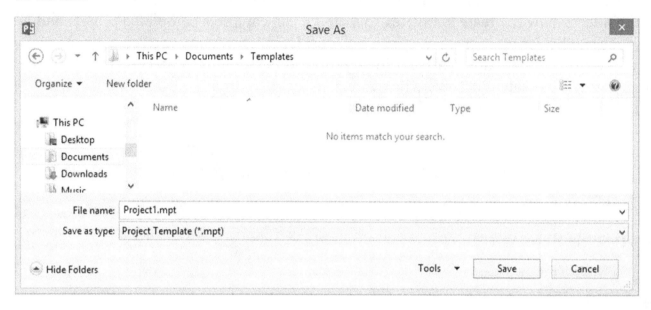

Step 4: In order to have the template available when creating new Project plans, you will want to keep the template location in the Microsoft/Templates folder that comes up by default.

Step 5: Select **Save**.

Creating a Project from an Existing Project
To create a new project from an existing project, use the following procedure.

Step 1: Select **File** from the Ribbon to open the Backstage View.

Step 2: Select **New**.

Step 3: Select **New from Existing Project**.

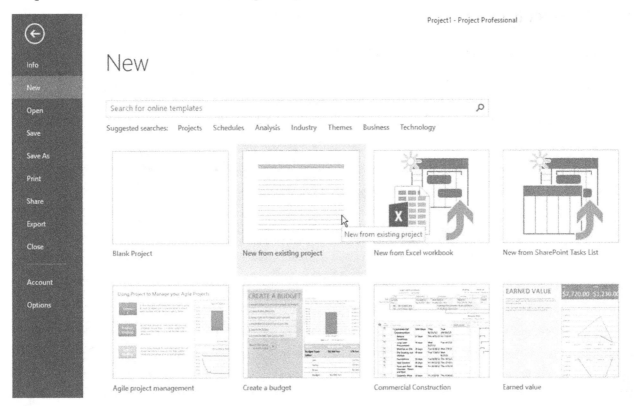

Step 4: In the *New From Existing Project* dialog box, navigate to the project you want to use to start the new project.

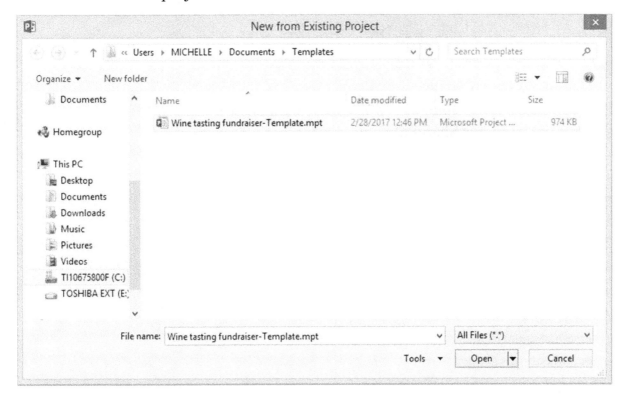

Step 5: Select **Create New**.

Creating a Project from a Microsoft SharePoint Task List

To create a project from a Microsoft SharePoint task list, use the following procedure.

Step 1: Select **File** from the Ribbon to open the Backstage View.

Step 2: Select **New**.

Step 3: Select **New from SharePoint task list**.

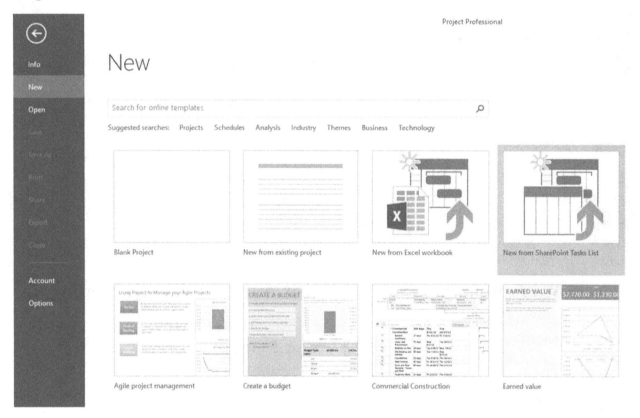

Step 4. In the *Import SharePoint Tasks List* dialog box, enter (or select from the drop down list) the **URL** for your SharePoint site.

Step 5: Select **Validate** to check the URL.

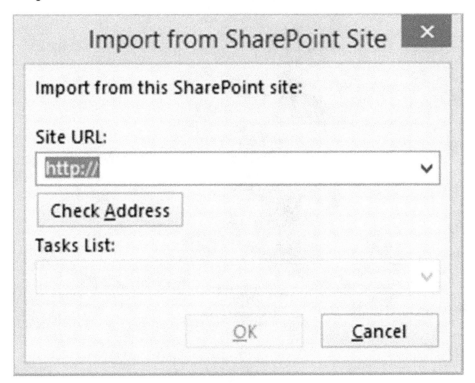

Step 6: Once you have validated the URL, you can choose a **Task List** from the drop down list to use your project plan.

Step 7: Select **OK**.

Creating a Project from a Microsoft Excel Workbook

To create a project from a Microsoft Excel workbook, use the following procedure.

Step 1: Select **File** from the Ribbon to open the Backstage View.

Step 2: Select **New**.

Step 3: Select **New from Excel Workbook**.

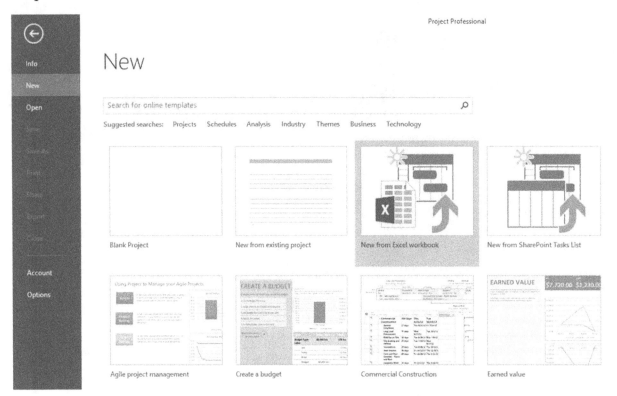

Step 4: In the *Open* dialog box, navigate to the location of the file you want to use and select **Open**.

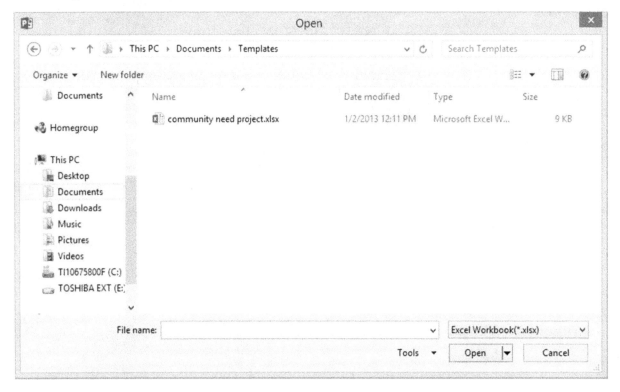

Step 5: In the *Import Wizard* dialog box, select **Next**.

Step 6: Select whether to use an existing Map or a New Map. For the purposes of this example, we will select **New Map.** Select **Next**.

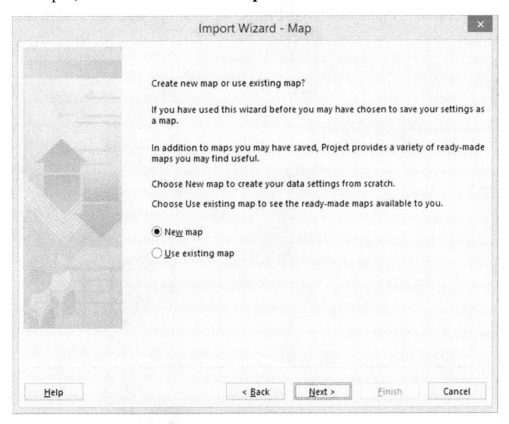

Step 7: Select the option to import the data **As a New Project**.

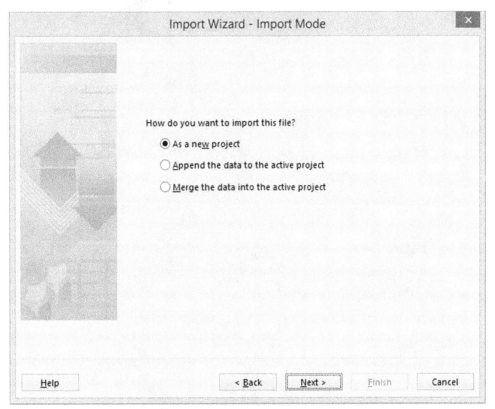

Step 8: The next screen on the *Import Wizard* allows you to indicate what type of information the Excel file includes. Our example only includes a few tasks and resources, so check **Tasks** and **Resources**, as well as the Import includes headers, and uncheck the other boxes. Select **Next**.

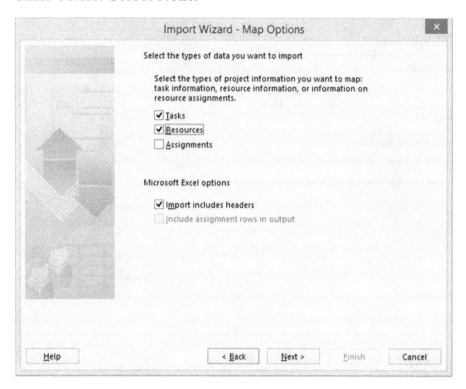

Step 9: The next screen on the *Import Wizard* maps the actual Excel workbook columns to Project fields for the TASKS only.

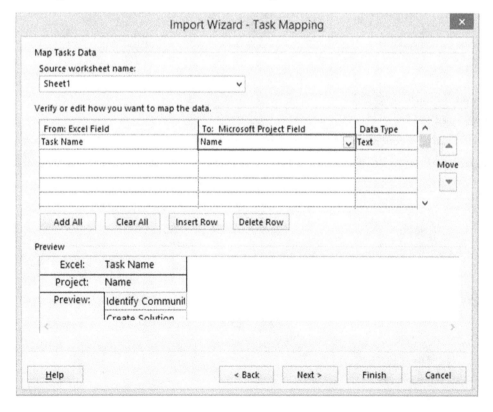

Select the **Source Worksheet** name from the drop down list.

- For each column in the **Excel** worksheet, select a column name from the drop down list in the first column of the Task mapping dialog box. Then select a **Microsoft Project Field** from the drop down list.

- You can use the up and down arrows to rearrange the order of the items.

- You can use **Add All**, **Clear All**, **Insert Row**, and **Delete Row** to manage the mapping information.

- Continue until you have mapped all of the TASK information from the Excel workbook to Microsoft Project fields.

- Select **Next**.

Step 10: The next screen on the *Import Wizard* maps the actual Excel workbook columns to Project fields for the RESOURCES only.

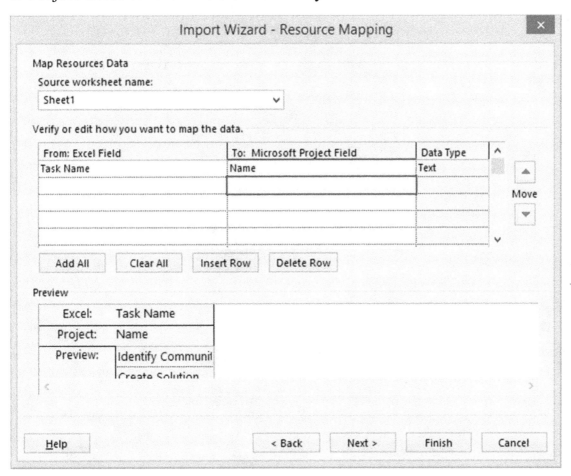

Select the **Source Worksheet** name from the drop down list.

- For each column in the **Excel** worksheet, select a column name from the drop down list in the first column of the Resource mapping dialog box. Then select a **Microsoft Project Field** from the drop down list.

- You can use the up and down arrows to rearrange the order of the items.

- You can use **Add All**, **Clear All**, **Insert Row**, and **Delete Row** to manage the mapping information.

- Continue until you have mapped all of the RESOURCE information from the Excel workbook to Microsoft Project fields.

- Select **Next**.

Step 11: On the final screen of the Import wizard, you can save your map for future use, or simply select **Finish**.

Chapter 4 – Working with Custom Fields

This chapter introduces you to the ability to customize a field for a specific use. You will first lean about custom fields. Then you will learn the general procedure for creating a custom field. We will look in depth at using a lookup table and creating formulas, as well as determining graphical indicator criteria. You will learn how to import a custom field from another project to save time. You will also learn how to show that custom field once you have created it.

About Custom Field Types

There are a number of fields available in Project 2013 that you can customize to meet your organization's needs.

You can use formulas, specific value calculations, or graphical indicators, among other customizations to make the fields work for you. Formula fields can include references to other fields. You can also create a list of values for a custom field to ensure fast and accurate data entry. You can use graphical indicators instead of data so that you can quickly see when data in that field meets certain criteria.

Creating a Custom Field

To customize a field, use the following procedure.

Step 1: Select the **Project** menu from the Ribbon. You can also get to this command from other tabs on the Ribbon.

Step 2: Select **Custom Fields**.

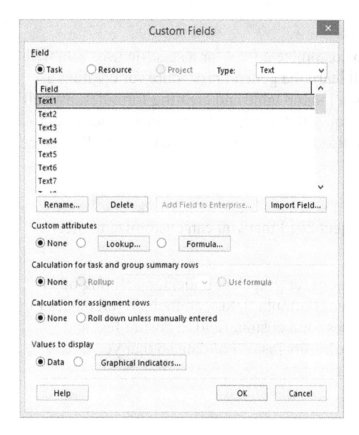

Step 3: Select whether the field will show in **Task** or **Resource** views.

Step 4: Select the **Type** of field from the drop down list.

Step 5: Highlight the field that you want to customize in the **Field** list. Each type of field has several customizable fields available.

Step 6: Select **Rename** to permanently rename the field. Enter the new name and select **OK**.

Step 7: Indicate the **Custom Attributes**, if any. We will talk more about lookup tables and formulas in the next two lessons.

Step 8: If you are customizing some types of fields, you can indicate a method of rolling up task and group summary values. This determines how values are summarized at the task and group summary levels. Outline codes and text fields do not roll up. The Use Formula option is available if you defined a formula under Custom Attributes.

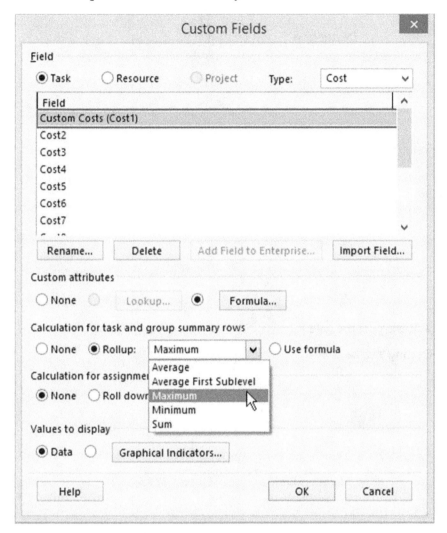

Step 9: Indicate how to calculate assignment rows. None indicates that contents of the custom field are not to be distributed across assignments. Roll down unless manually entered indicates to distribute the contents across assignments.

Step 10: Indicate whether to display values or graphical indicators. We will talk more about graphical indicators later in this chapter.

Step 11: Select **OK** to save the changes to your field.

Using a Lookup Table

To create a lookup table for a custom field, use the following procedure.

Step 1: Prepare a custom field as defined in the previous lesson, steps 1-6.

Step 2: Select **Lookup**.

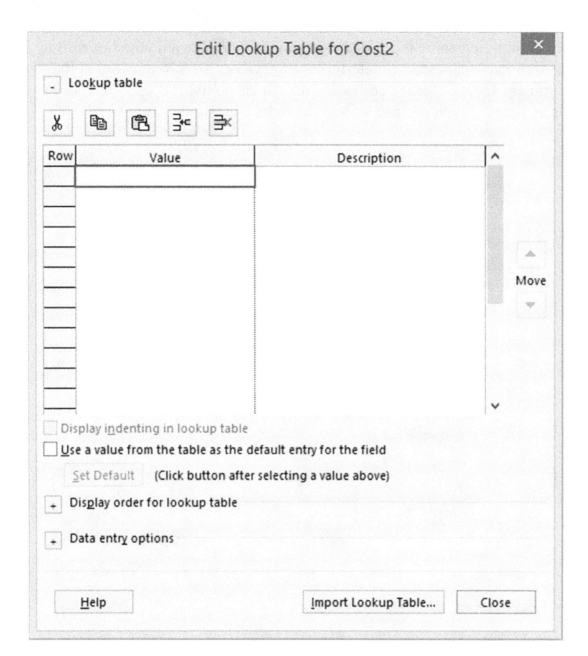

Step3: Enter each list item in the **Value** column. You can also enter a **Description** for the value.

The tools at the top of the dialog box allow you to cut, copy, paste, insert, or delete a row. You can also use the Move up or down arrows to rearrange your list.

Step 4: If you want a default value to appear in the field for your list, highlight the value you want to use, check the **Use a value** box, and select **Set Default**.

Step 5: You can choose a display order for your values. Select the plus sign next to **Display Order** and choose **By Row Number**, **Sort Ascending,** or **Sort Descending**.

Step 6: To allow new values to be added during data entry, select the plus sign next to **Data Entry** Options and check the **Allow Additional Items** box.

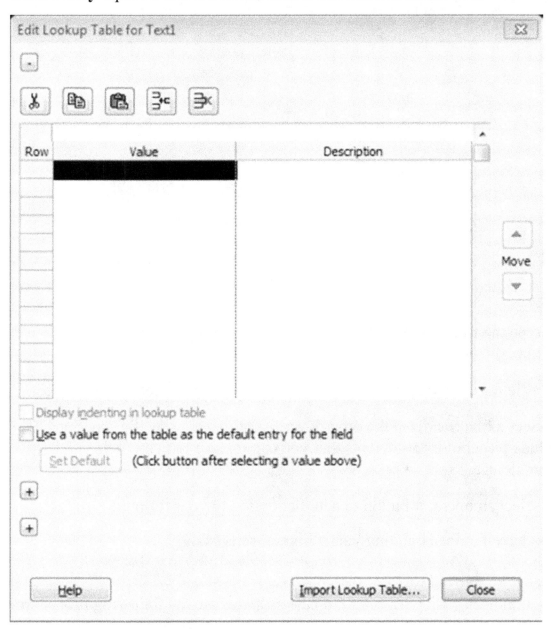

Creating Basic Formulas

To create a basic formula for a custom field, use the following procedure.

Step 1: Prepare a custom field as defined in the custom field lesson, steps 1-6.

Step 2: Select **Formula**.

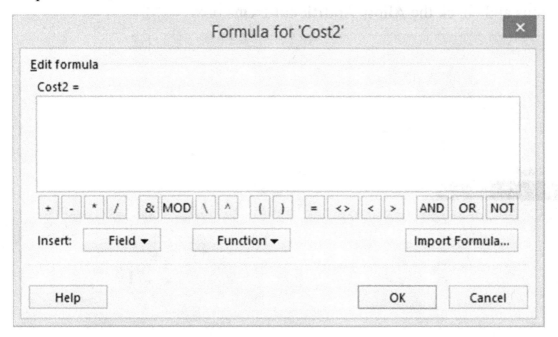

Step 3: You can type the formula in the box, or use the following building blocks to create your formula:

- **Field**– select a field from the drop down list to reference another field in the project.

- **Function** – select a function from the drop down list to insert a specific function. The functions include placeholder arguments that you can replace with the fields and values you want to use.

- **Operators** – select an operator button to add that option to your formula.

Step 4: When you have finished building your formula, select **OK**.

Determining Graphical Indicator Criteria

To create graphical indicator with criteria for a custom field, use the following procedure.

Step 1: Prepare a custom field as defined in the custom field lesson, steps 1-6.

Step 2: Select **Graphical Indicators**.

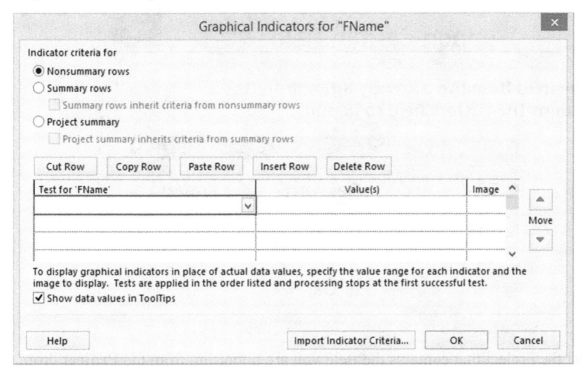

Step 3: Under Indicator criteria for, select either **Non summary rows**, **Summary rows**, or **Project summary**. If you do not want summary rows or the project summary to inherit test criteria, deselect the corresponding check box.

Step 4: Select a test from the drop down list (or enter your own) to indicate the criteria for the custom field.

Step 5: Select the value to use for the criteria from the drop down list to indicate the field where the value is located. You can also enter your own value to use a specific value instead of a value referenced from another field. Project will compare the test to the value in the custom field.

Step 6: Select an Image from the drop down list to indicate the image you want to display as a result of the test.

Step 7: Repeat steps 4 – 6 to apply additional tests to the custom field.

Step 8: The tools at the top of the dialog box allow you to cut, copy, paste, insert, or delete a row. You can also use the Move up or down arrows to rearrange your list. The tests are applied in order from top to bottom.

Importing a Custom Field

To import a custom field, use the following procedure.

Step 1: Select the **Project** menu from the Ribbon. You can also get to this command from other tabs on the Ribbon.

Step 2: Select **Custom Fields**.

Step 3: Select **Import Field**.

Import Custom Field

Select the field from the currently open projects that contains the custom field to import:

Project: Global.MPT

Field type: ● T**a**sk   ○ **R**esource   ○ Pro**j**ect

Field: Cost1

OK   Cancel

Step 4: Select the project that contains the field you are importing from the **Project** drop down list. The other project should be open.

Step 5: Select the type of field as **Task**, **Resource**, or **Project**.

Step 6: Select the name of the field you are importing from the **Field** drop down list.

Step 7: Select **OK**.

Inserting a Custom Field

To insert a custom field into a view, use the following procedure.

Step 1: Your new field will be inserted to the left of the column you select. Select the appropriate column header.

Step 2: Select the **Format** tab from the Ribbon.

Step 3: Select **Insert Column**.

Step 4: Begin typing the name of the field or simply select it from the list.

[Type Column Name]

Start

% Complete
% Work Complete
Active
Actual Cost
Actual Duration
Actual Finish
Actual Overtime Cost
Actual Overtime Work
Actual Start
Actual Work
ACWP
Assignment
Assignment Delay
Assignment Owner
Assignment Units
Baseline Budget Cost
Baseline Budget Work
Baseline Cost
Baseline Deliverable Finish
Baseline Deliverable Start
Baseline Duration
Baseline Estimated Duration
Baseline Estimated Finish
Baseline Estimated Start
Baseline Finish
Baseline Fixed Cost
Baseline Fixed Cost Accrual
Baseline Start
Baseline Work
Baseline1 Budget Cost
Baseline1 Budget Work
Baseline1 Cost
Baseline1 Deliverable Finish
Baseline1 Deliverable Start
Baseline1 Duration
Baseline1 Estimated Duration
Baseline1 Estimated Finish
Baseline1 Estimated Start
Baseline1 Finish
Baseline1 Fixed Cost
Baseline1 Fixed Cost Accrual
Baseline1 Start
Baseline1 Work
Baseline10 Budget Cost
Baseline10 Budget Work
Baseline10 Cost
Baseline10 Deliverable Finish
Baseline10 Deliverable Start

Chapter 5 – Working with Tasks

This chapter will teach you some additional ways to work with tasks. First, you will learn how to display the Project Summary task in order to get a high-level view of the duration, start and end dates for your project (as well as any other columns of information you may be viewing). You will also learn how to create milestones. If your plan needs a little tweaking, you may want to rearrange your tasks or cancel them. This chapter also explains how to create manually scheduled tasks. Finally, you will learn how to create a recurring task.

Displaying the Project Summary Task on a New Project

To display the project summary task, use the following procedure.

Step 1: Select the **Format** tab from the Ribbon.

Step 2: Check the **Project Summary Task** box.

Creating Milestones

To create a milestone, use the following procedure.

Step 1: On the empty row in the Gantt Chart view, enter the name of the milestone.

Step 2: Enter 0 as the duration.

To create a milestone for a task with a duration longer than 0, use the following procedure.

Step 1: Enter the task name and duration as you would for any new task.

Step 2: Double-click the task to open the Task information dialog box.

Step 3: Select the Advanced tab.

Step 4: Check the **Mark Task as Milestone** box.

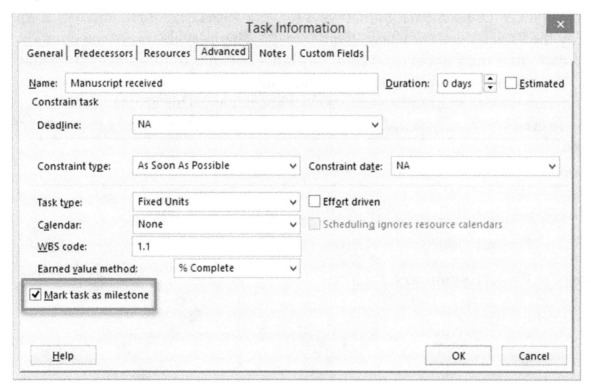

Step 5: Select **OK**.

Rearranging Tasks

To rearrange a single task, use the following procedure.

Step 1: Select the task that you want to rearrange.

Step 2: Drag it to the new location. The task is shown as a horizontal bar until you release the mouse button.

3	✓	🖱	Content edit	29 days	Wed 7/11/12	Wed 8/22/12	2		Carole Poland	
4	✓	🖱	Handoff to Editorial	0 days	Wed 8/22/12	Wed 8/22/12	3		Carole Poland	
5		🖱	◢ Editorial	30 days	Thu 8/23/12	Wed 10/3/12	1			
6		🖱	Organize manuscript for copyedit	5 days	Thu 8/23/12	Wed 8/29/12			Robin Wood	
7		🖱	Copyedit	20 days	Thu 8/30/12	Wed 9/26/12	6		Copyeditors	
8		🖱	Copyedit incorp	5 days	Thu 9/27/12	Wed 10/3/12	7		Robin Wood	
9		🖱	Handoff to	0 days	Wed 10/3/12	Wed 10/3/12	8		Robin Wood	

To rearrange a summary task, use the following procedure.

Step 1: Select the summary task that you want to rearrange.

Step 2: Drag it to the new location. The group is shown as a horizontal bar until you release the mouse button.

1	✓	⬛	⊿ Acquisition	31 days	Wed 7/11/12	Wed 8/22/12		
2	✓	⬛	Manuscript received	0 days	Wed 7/11/12	Wed 7/11/12		Carole Poland
3	✓	⬛	Content edit	29 days	Wed 7/11/12	Wed 8/22/12	2	Carole Poland
4		⬛	⊿ Editorial	30 days	Wed 8/22/12	Wed 10/3/12	1	
5		⬛	Organize manuscript for copyedit	5 days	Thu 8/23/12	Wed 8/29/12		Robin Wood
6	✓	⬛	Handoff to Editorial	0 days	Wed 8/22/12	Wed 8/22/12	3	Carole Poland

Canceling an Unneeded Task

To delete a task, use the following procedure.

Step 1: Right click on the task you want to remove from the project plan.

Step 2: Select **Delete** from the context menu.

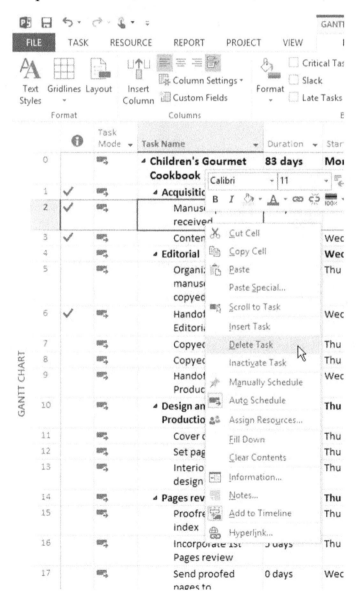

43

The task is removed.

To inactivate a task, use the following procedure.

Step 1: Highlight the task in the project plan.

Step 2: Select Inactivate from the Task tab on the Ribbon.

The task is crossed out to show that it is inactive.

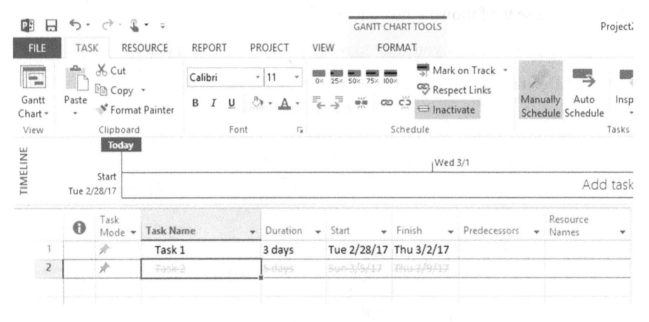

Creating Manually Scheduled Tasks

To change an existing task to be manually scheduled, use the following procedure.

Step 1: Select the task that you want to change in the Gant chart view of the Project plan.

Step 2: Select **Manually Schedule.**

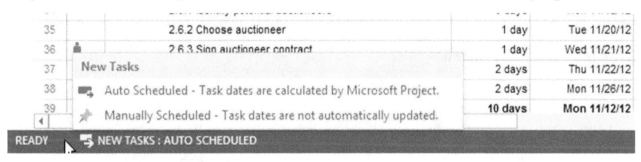

To change the default to manually schedule all new tasks, use the following procedure.

Step 1: On the Status Bar at the bottom of the screen, select the **New Tasks: Auto Scheduled** notification.

Step 2: Select **Manually Scheduled – Task dates are not automatically updated**.

35		2.6.2 Choose auctioneer	1 day	Tue 11/20/12
36		2.6.3 Sign auctioneer contract	1 day	Wed 11/21/12
37	New Tasks		2 days	Thu 11/22/12
38	Auto Scheduled - Task dates are calculated by Microsoft Project.		2 days	Mon 11/26/12
39	Manually Scheduled - Task dates are not automatically updated.		10 days	Mon 11/12/12

READY   NEW TASKS : AUTO SCHEDULED

Creating a Recurring Task

To create a recurring task, use the following procedure.

Step 1: Select the row on the Gantt chart view of the Project plan where you want the recurring task to appear.

Step 2: On the **Task** tab of the Ribbon, select the arrow below the Task tool in the Insert group.

Step 3: Select **Recurring Task**.

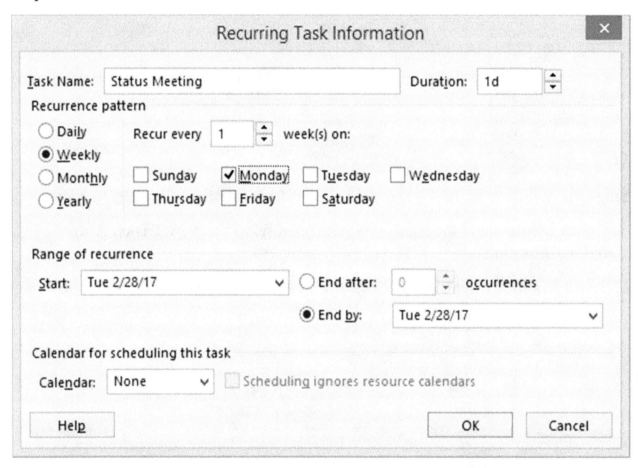

Step 4: In the *Recurring Task Information* dialog box, enter a **Task Name**.

Step 5: Enter the **Duration** for the task.

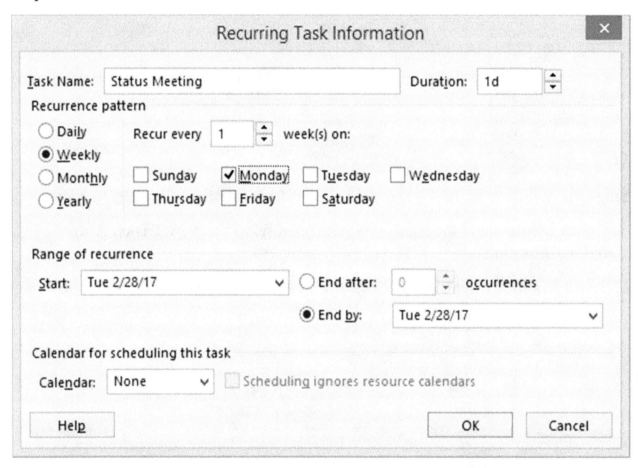

Step 6: Select which interval the task will repeat (Daily, Weekly, Monthly or Yearly). Depending on your selection, complete additional details for the recurrence pattern:

If you selected **Daily**, enter the number of days and whether it is every day or just work days.

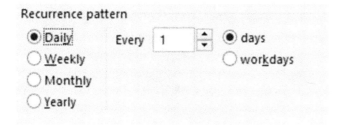

If you selected **Weekly**, enter the number of weeks and check the box(es) for the days of the weeks on which the task recurs.

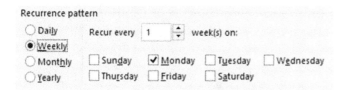

If you selected **Monthly**, select the pattern by date or by day of the week and which week.

If you selected **Yearly**, select the pattern by date or by day of the week and which week and which month.

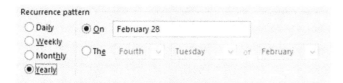

Step 1: For the **Range of Recurrence**, enter the **Start Date** and either the **End Date** or the number of occurrences to end after.

Step 2: Select a **Resource Calendar** from the drop down list.

Step 3: Select **OK**.

Chapter 6 – Working with Resources, Part 1

This chapter helps you handle resources in your projects. First, you will learn how to use the Assign Resources dialog box to both remove and replace a resource assignment. You will also learn how to manage unassigned tasks. Then, the chapter covers some options for resolving resource conflicts. You will also learn how to print a view or report of resource information.

Removing a Resource Assignment

To remove a resource assignment, use the following procedure.

Step 1: While in Gantt Chart view, select the task for which you want to remove a resource assignment.

Step 2: Select the **Resources** tab from the Ribbon.

Step 3: Select **Assign Resources**.

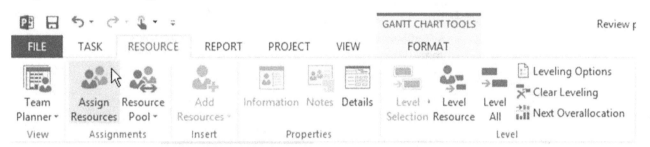

Step 4: In the *Assign Resources* dialog box, highlight the resource you want to remove. If there is more than one resource assigned, and you want to remove all of them, you can hold the SHIFT or CTRL keys down while selecting the resources.

Step 5: Select **Remove**.

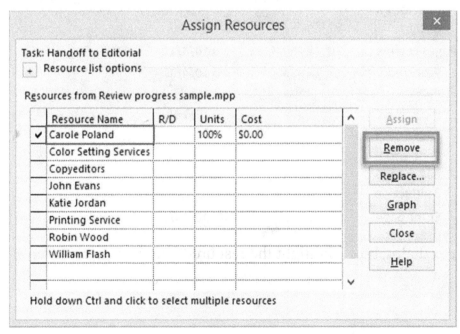

Replacing a Resource Assignment

To replace a resource, use the following procedure.

Step 1: While in Gantt Chart view, select the task for which you want to replace a resource assignment.

Step 2: Right-click the task.

Step 3: Select **Assign Resources** from the context menu.

			Cookbook		7/11/12
1	✓	➡	⊿ Acquisition	31 days	Wed 7/11/:
2	✓	➡	Manuscript received	0 days	Wed 7/11/1
3	✓	➡	Content ed		
4	✓	➡	Handoff to Editorial	0 days	Wed 8/22/1
5		➡	⊿ Editorial		8/23/1:
6		➡	Organize manuscrip copyedit		8/23/1:
7		➡	Copyedit		8/30/1:
8		➡	Copyedit i		9/27/1:
9		➡	Handoff to Production		10/3/1
10		➡	⊿ Design and Production		8/23/1:
11		➡	Cover desi		8/23/1:
12		➡	Set pages		8/30/1:
13		➡	Interior ill design		8/30/1:
14		➡	⊿ Pages review		10/4/1:
15		➡	Proofread index		10/4/1:
16		➡	Incorporat Pages revi		10/18/:
17		➡	Send proo pages to Production		10/24,
18		➡	Enter page	5 days	Thu 10/25/:

Context menu (overlaid):

Calibri · 11 ·

B *I* 🖊 · A · 🔗 🔗 🔲 · ⬇

- ✂ Cut Cell
- 🗐 Copy Cell
- 📋 Paste
- Paste Special...
- ➡ Scroll to Task
- Insert Task
- Delete Task
- Inactivate Task
- 📌 Manually Schedule
- ➡ Auto Schedule
- 👥 Assign Resources...
- Fill Down
- Clear Contents
- 🔳 Information...
- Notes...
- 🔳 Add to Timeline
- 🌐 Hyperlink...

GANTT CHART

Step 4: In the *Assign Resources* dialog box, highlight the resource you want to replace.

Step 5: Select **Replace**.

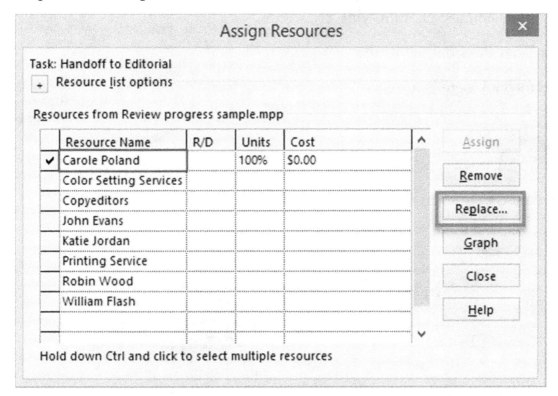

Step 6: In the *Replace Resources* dialog box, select the new resource to assign to the selected task.

Step 7: Select **OK**.

The Resource Usage Sheet, use the following procedure.

Step 1: Select the **View** tab from the Ribbon.

Step 2: Select **Resource Usage**.

Step 3: The *Resource Usage sheet* shows all of the unassigned tasks at the top of the sheet.

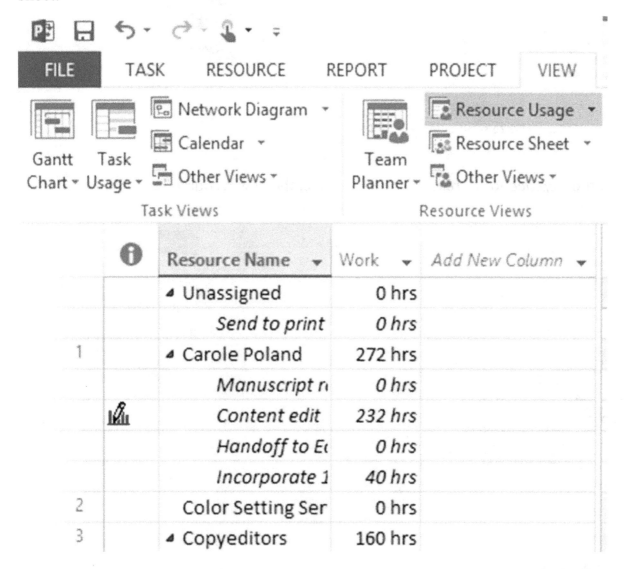

Step 4: You can use the **View** tools to help filter and manage the information.

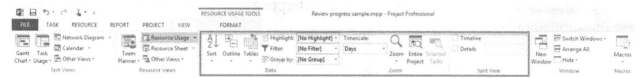

Step 5: You can also use the **Resource Usage Tools Format** tools to insert columns or custom fields, change the column settings, or choose which information to show on the right side of the screen.

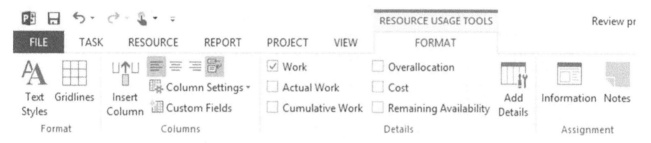

Step 6: You can also select **Information** to view the *Assignment information* dialog box.

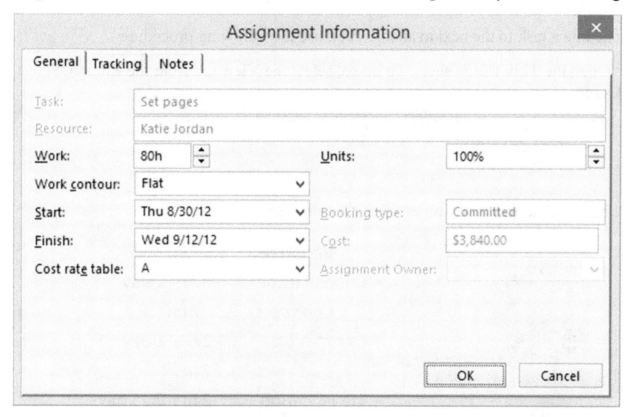

Another way to assign resources is by simply dragging the task assignment from one resource grouping to another. The task assignment appears as a horizontal bar until you release the mouse button.

		Proofread an	80 hrs		Work
5		◢ Katie Jordan	200 hrs		Work
		Set pages	80 hrs		Work
		Proofread an	80 hrs		Work
		Enter page cc	40 hrs		Work
6		Printing Service	0 hrs		Work
7		◢ Robin Wood	200 hrs		Work
		Organize mai	40 hrs		Work
		Copyedit incc	40 hrs		Work
		Handoff to P	0 hrs		Work

RESOURCE USAGE

Resolving Resource Conflicts

To reschedule a task to the next available date, use the following procedure.

Step 1: Open the Task Usage sheet. To do so, select the **View** tab from the Ribbon. Select **Task Usage**.

Step 2: Right-click on a task with an over allocation icon.

			Voluntee	8 hrs	
8			◢ Choose locat	8 hrs	1 day
			Chairpers	8 hrs	
9			◢ Reserve locat	2 hrs	1 day
		This task has overallocated resources. Right-click for options.	...ers	2 hrs	
10			◢ Sign location	2 hrs	0.25 days
			Chairpers	2 hrs	

TASK USAGE

Step 3: Select **Reschedule to Available Date** from the context menu.

8	B I 🖌 ▾ **A** ▾ ∞ ⟳ ▅ ▾ ⬇	cat	8 hrs
		chuipers	*8 hrs*
9	? Fix in Task Inspector...	⟩cat	2 hrs
		ers	*2 hrs*
10	Reschedule to Available Date ⬉	on	2 hrs
	Ignore Problems for This Task	*ers*	*2 hrs*
11	✂ Cut Cell		**6 hrs**
12	📋 Copy Cell	uor	2 hrs
	Paste	*ers*	*2 hrs*
13	Paste Special...	altl	2 hrs
		ers	*2 hrs*
14	Scroll to Task	ota	0 hrs
15	Insert Task	its	2 hrs
	Delete Task	tee	2 hrs
16	Inactivate Task	ice	28.8 hrs
17	Manually Schedule	rint	4.8 hrs
		Stc	*4.8 hrs*
18	Auto Schedule	ote	8 hrs
	Assign Resources...	tee	*8 hrs*
19	Fill Down	int	8 hrs
	Clear Contents	ity	*8 hrs*
20	Information...	ng	8 hrs
		ers	*8 hrs*
21	Notes...		**28 hrs**
22	Add to Timeline	ote	8 hrs
	Hyperlink...	tee	*8 hrs*
23		◢ Request prop	2 hrs
		Voluntee	*2 hrs*

TASK USAGE

Step 4: The selected task is rescheduled.

Remember that you can use the Clear Leveling Options on the Resource tab if you need to revert to the schedule before you have done any leveling (either by task or for the whole project).

The Task Inspector pane.

Step 1: Task Usage sheet. To do so, select the **View** tab from the Ribbon. Select **Task Usage**.

Step 2: Right-click on a task with an over allocation icon.

Step 3: Select **Fix in Task Inspector** from the context menu.

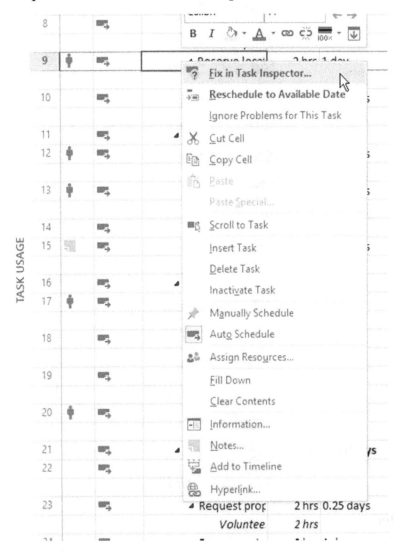

The Task Inspector pane opens on the left side of the screen.

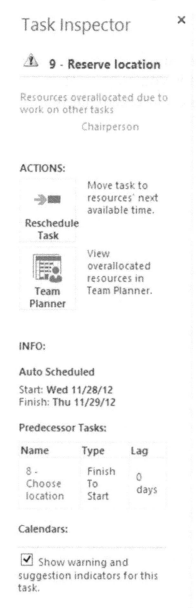

Use the scroll bar to see all of the options in the Task Inspector pane.

You can Reschedule the selected task; view the over allocated resources in the Team Planner, or see the factors affecting the task.

Printing a View or Report of Resource Information

To print a resource view, use the following procedure.

Step 1: Open the view that you want to print. For this example, let us use the Resource Usage view.

Step 2: Select the **File** tab from the Ribbon to open the Backstage view.

Step 3: Select **Print**.

Step 4: Use the Print Preview area to review your selection. For example, notice that the Resource Usage view is 96 pages when you print all dates. Perhaps you only want to print a week or a month of this view. You can use the **Date Range** settings to adjust.

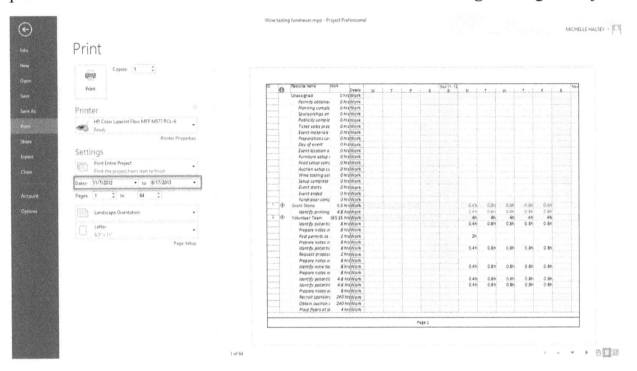

Step 5: Select **Print**.

To print a resource report, use the following procedure.

Step 1: Select the **Project** tab from the Ribbon.

Step 2: Select **Reports**.

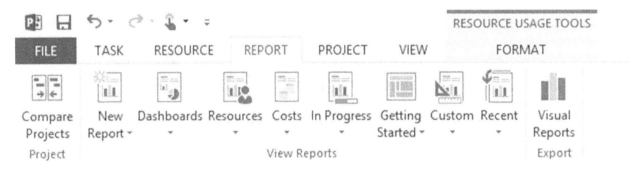

Step 3: In the *Reports* dialog box, select the report category you want to print. Click **Select**.

Step 4: In the dialog box for the report category you chose, select the report that you want to print and click **Select**.

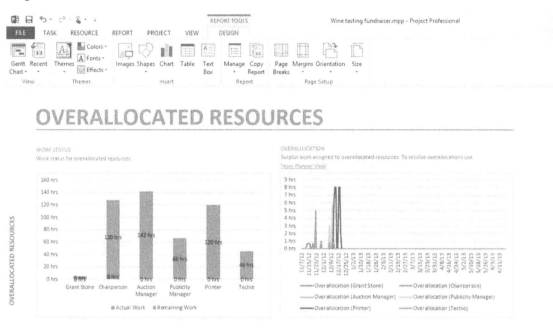

Step 5: Use the Print Preview area to adjust your settings, if necessary.

Step 6: Select **Print**.

Chapter 7, Working with Resources, Part 2

You learn even more resource procedures in this chapter. We will talk about adding individual and multiple resources to the Enterprise Resource Pool so that you can share resources from your project with the entire organization. You will also learn how to export and import resource information to or from other file formats, like Microsoft Excel. Finally, you will learn how to view resource availability across multiple projects.

Adding Resources to the Enterprise Resource Pool

To add individual resources to the enterprise resource pool, use the following procedure.

Step 1: Select the **Resources** tab from the Ribbon.

Step 2: Select **Resource Pool.** Select **Enterprise Resource Pool.**

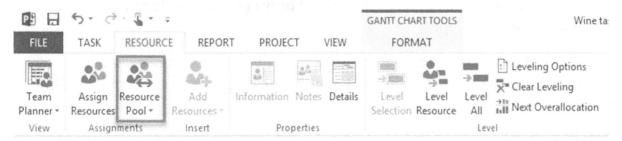

Step 3: Your browser displays Project Web Access. Check to see if it is not the window shown on top.

Step 4: On Project Web Access, select **New Resource**.

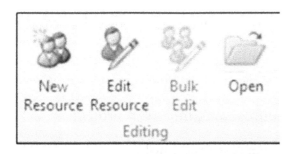

Step 5: Enter the resource information.

- Select **work resource, cost resource**, or **material resource** from the **Resource Type** list.

- Check the **Budget** or **Generic** check box to indicate that the resource is a budget resource or a generic (placeholder or skill based) resource.

- Clear the **Resource can log on to Project Server** check box if you do not want to collect information on tasks that the resource works on, or if you do not want the resource to log on to Microsoft Project Server.

- Enter the **Resource Name** and other identifying information, including the resource's email address and Resource Breakdown Structure value. You can also enter the hyperlink name and URL if the resource maintains a team website.

- Clear the **Leveling** box to exclude the resource from leveling in Project.

- In the **Timesheet manager** box, enter or search for the manager's name if the resource is a timesheet manager.

- In the **Default Assignment Owner** box, enter or search for the assignment owner's name to indicate an assignment owner for this resource.

Step 6: Indicate the resource's **Base Calendar**.

Step 7: Indicate whether the resource is committed or proposed by selecting an option from the **Default Booking Type**.

Step 8: Check the **Team Assignment Pool** to indicate that the resource is a member of a team and enter the name of the team in the **Team Name** box. (Or select Browse to find the name of the team.)

Step 9: Use the calendar icon to change the **Earliest Available** and **Latest Available** dates for the resource.

Step 10: Select the **Group**, **Code**, **Cost Center** and **Cost Type** codes for the resource, if applicable.

Step 11: Enter any additional information about the resource that your organization requires in the **Resource Custom Fields**.

Step 12: Select **Save**.

Remember that you will need to add the enterprise resource back into your project.

You can also import multiple resources into the enterprise resource pool at once. To import multiple resources, use the following procedure.

Step 1: Select the **Resources** tab from the Ribbon.

Step 2: Select **Add Resources**. Select **Import Resources to Enterprise**.

Project displays the Import Resources wizard on the left with the Resource Sheet view on the right.

Step 1: For each resource that you want to import, select **Yes** in the corresponding **Import** column.

Step 2: If you have customized field, select **Map Resource Fields** to map the custom fields in your project with enterprise custom fields defined by your organization.

Step 3: Select **Continue to Step 2** to validate information about the resources and ensure that no errors are created when the resources are imported. If there are errors, they are displayed next to the resource name in the **Errors** column.

Step 4: Select **Save and Finish**.

Exporting Resource Data

To export resource information, use the following procedure.

Step 1: Select the **File** tab from the Ribbon.

Step 2: Select **Save As**.

Step 3: In the *Save As* dialog box, select the file format you want to use for the export from the **Save As Type** drop down list.

Step 4: Enter the **File Name**.

Step 5: Select **Save**.

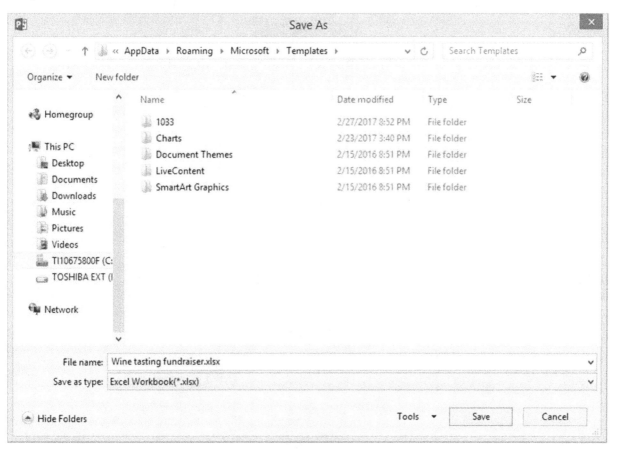

Project opens the *Export Wizard* to export the data you want into the proper fields for the destination file.

Step 6: Select **Selected Data**. Select **Next**.

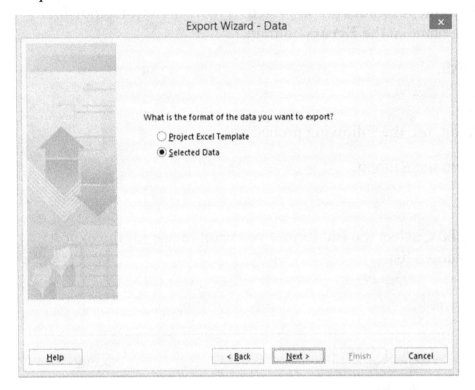

Step 7: Select **New map** unless you have previously saved a map file. Select **Next**.

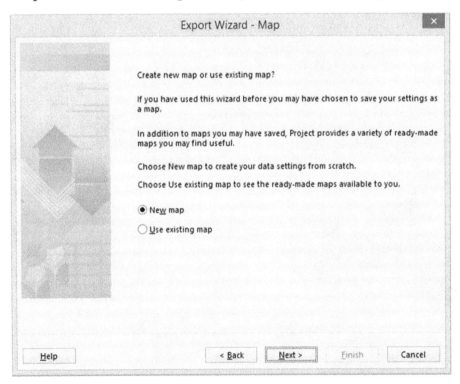

Step 8: Check the **Resources** box. If desired, select **Include assignment rows in output**. Select **Next**.

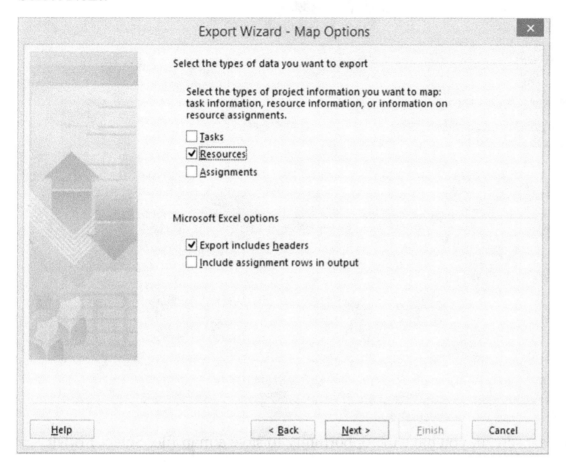

Step 9: On the *Resource Mapping* screen, complete the following steps:

Step 9a: Enter the **Destination Worksheet name** for the destination worksheet, if you want to change it.

Step 9b: Select the **Export Filter** from the drop down list, if you want to change it.

Step 9c: For each **Microsoft Project Field**, select a column name from the drop down list in the first column of the *Resource mapping* dialog box. Then enter a heading in the **Excel Field** column.

Step 9d: You can use the up and down arrows to rearrange the order of the items.

Step 9e: You can use **Add All**, **Clear All**, **Insert Row**, and **Delete Row** to manage the mapping information.

Step 9f: Continue until you have mapped all of the RESOURCE information from Microsoft Project to Excel workbook to fields.

Step 9g: Select **Next**.

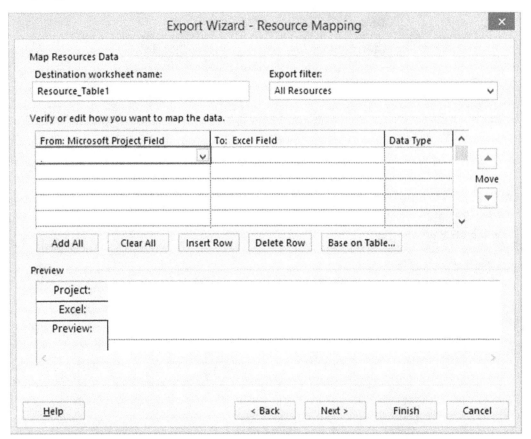

Step 10: On the last screen, you have the opportunity to save a map file. Select **Finish**.

Importing Resource Data

To import resource information, use the following procedure.

Step 1: Select the **File** tab to open the Backstage View.

Step 2: Select **Open**.

Step 3: In the *Open* dialog box, select the type of file you want to import from the drop down list next to **File Name**. In this example, we will choose **Excel Workbook**.

Step 4: Select the **File** you want to import.

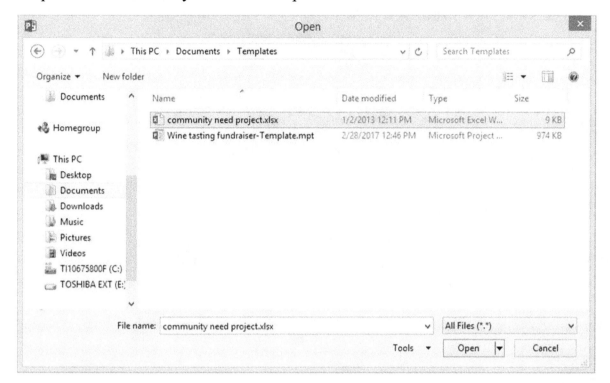

Step 5: Select **Open**.

Step 6: In the *Import Wizard* dialog box, select **Next**.

Step 7: Select whether to use an existing Map or a New Map. For the purposes of this example, we will select **New Map.** Select **Next**.

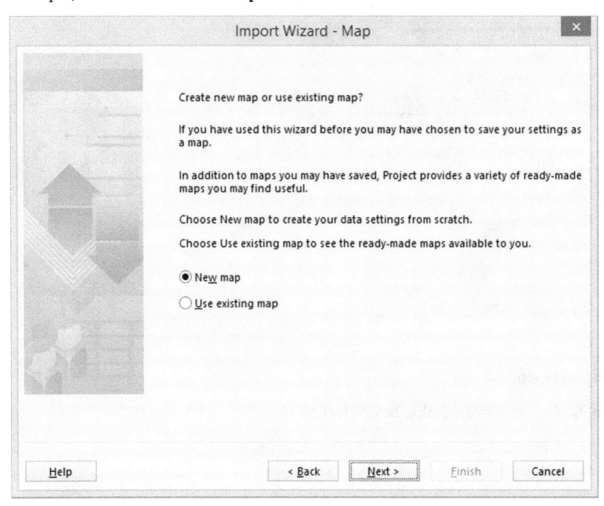

Step 8: Select the option to import the data either to **Append the Data to the Active Project**, or if have some of the resource information already in your project and you want to add missing details or additional resources, select **Merge the Data to the Active project**.

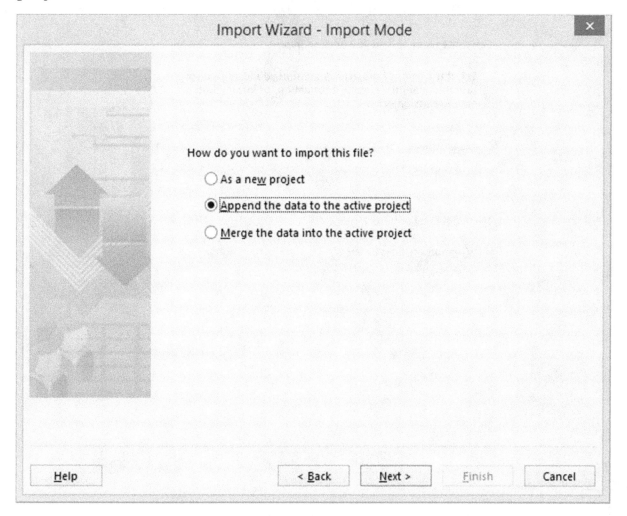

69

Step 9: The next screen on the *Import Wizard* allows you to indicate what type of information the Excel file includes. Check the **Resources** box as well as the Import includes headers. Select **Next**.

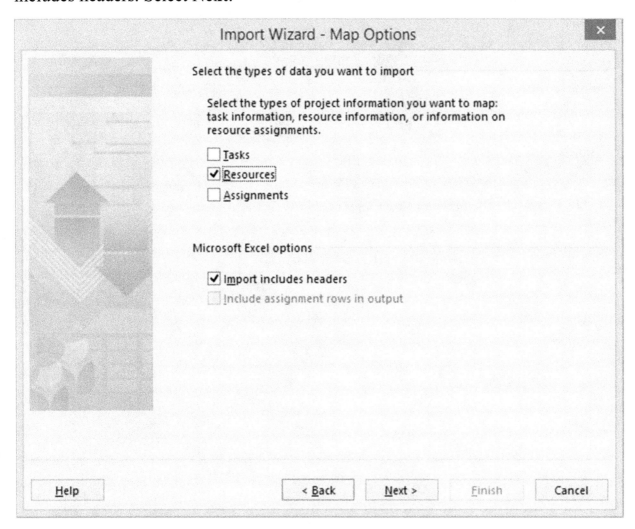

Step 10: The next screen on the *Import Wizard* maps the actual Excel workbook columns to Project fields for the RESOURCES.

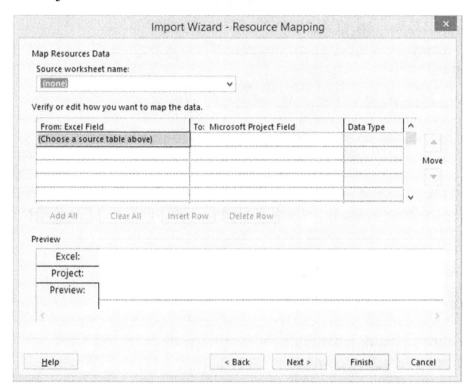

- Select the **Source Worksheet** name from the drop down list.

- For each column in the **Excel** worksheet, select a column name from the drop down list in the first column of the Resource mapping dialog box. Then select a **Microsoft Project Field** from the drop down list.

- You can use the up and down arrows to rearrange the order of the items.

- You can use **Add All**, **Clear All**, **Insert Row**, and **Delete Row** to manage the mapping information.

- Continue until you have mapped all of the RESOURCE information from the Excel workbook to Microsoft Project fields.

- Select **Next**.

Step 11: On the final screen of the Import wizard, you can save your map for future use, or simply select **Finish**.

To change enterprise resource information, use the following procedure.

Step 1: Select the **Resource** tab from the Ribbon.

Step 2: Select **Resource Pool**

Step 3: Select **Enterprise Resource Pool**.

The **Resource Center** opens in Internet Explorer, displaying a list of the enterprise resources.

Step 4: Check the box next to the resource you want to modify and select **Edit Resource**. You can also select multiple resources and select **Bulk Edit** to make the same changes to more than one resource.

Step 5: Change the resource information as needed.

Step 6: Select **Save**.

If you need to change the resource calendar, availability, contours, or cost, you must make the changes in the enterprise resource pool

To make changes in the enterprise resource pool for these types of changes, use the following procedure.

Step 1: Select the **Resource** tab from the Ribbon.

Step 2: Select **Resource Pool**

Step 3: Select **Enterprise Resource Pool**.

The **Resource Center** opens in Internet Explorer, displaying a list of the enterprise resources.

Step 4: Check the box next to the resource(s) you want to modify and select **Open**.

A new project opens with the selected resources displayed in the Resource Sheet Tools view.

Step 5: Update the resource information as needed.

Step 6: Select the **File** tab from the Ribbon.

Step 7: Select **Save**.

Viewing Availability Across Multiple Projects

To view resource usage for a resource who has been assigned tasks for multiple projects, use the following procedure.

Step 1: We will use the SampleMulti project.

Step 2: Open the **Resource Usage** view.

Step 3: Scroll down to the resource named Grant Stone.

All tasks from projects that share resources are shown with the resource's name.

	ⓘ	Resource Name	Work	Add New Column	Details	F	S	S	M	T	W	T	F	S
1		▲ Grant Stone	0.47 hrs		Work						0.15h	0.15h	0.15h	
		Task A	0.23 hrs		Work						0.08h	0.08h	0.08h	
		Task B	0.23 hrs		Work						0.08h	0.08h	0.08h	
					Work									
					Work									
					Work									
					Work									
					Work									
					Work									
					Work									
					Work									
					Work									
					Work									

(Nov 4, '12)

You can also view the details for a resource, including all assignments from multiple projects.

Step 1: Select the **Resource** tab from the Ribbon.

Step 2: Select **Details**.

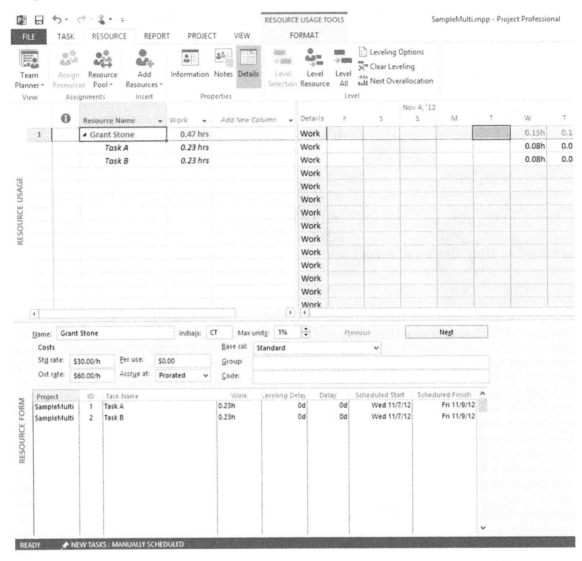

Notice in the details area at the bottom, the project name for each task is listed on the left.

Chapter 8 – Using the Team Planner

This chapter focuses on formatting the Team Planner view so that you can customize the way the information is shown. First, we will look at how to roll up tasks so that you can control the amount of detail shown on the Team Planner. Next, you will learn how to work with the Team Planner gridlines. You will also learn how to change the text styles. You can change the fill and border styles for several different types of tasks, so that you can differentiate each type of task at a glance. This chapter also explains how to prevent over allocations when making changes in the Team Planner view. Finally, we will look at how to show or hide unassigned and unscheduled tasks.

Rolling Up Tasks

To roll up task information, use the following procedure.

Step 1: Switch to the Team Planner view by selecting **Team Planner** from the **View** tab on the Ribbon.

Step 2: Select the **Team Planner Tools Format** tab from the Ribbon.

Step 3: Select **Rollup**.

Step 4: Select the level of details you would like to view.

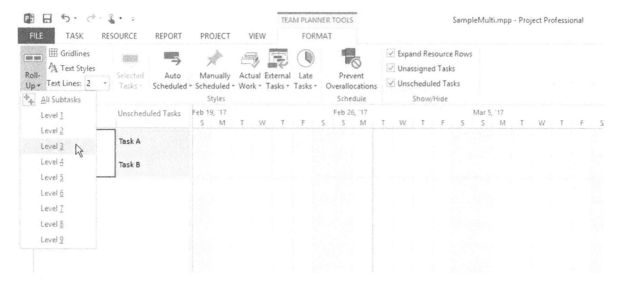

Working with Gridlines

To format gridlines on the Team Planner, use the following procedure.

Step 1: Select the **Team Planner Tools Format** tab from the Ribbon.

Step 2: Select **Gridlines**.

Step 3: In the *Gridlines* dialog box, select which line you want to change.

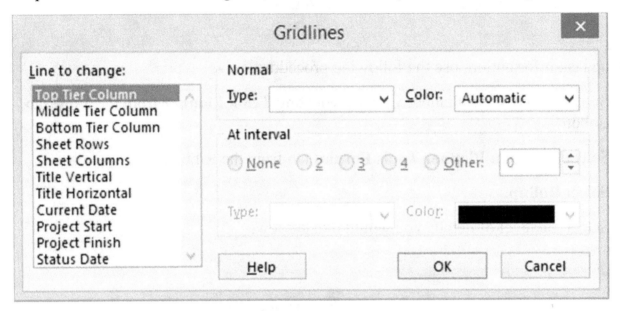

Step 4: Select the **Type** of gridline you want to use for the selected line from the drop down list.

Step 5: Select the **Color** for the selected line from the drop down list.

Step 6: When you are using Sheet Rows, you can have another type and color for various intervals. Select **None, 2, 3, 4,** or **Other** and enter the number of rows. Select the **Type** of gridline from the drop down list. Select the **Color** for the gridline from the drop down list.

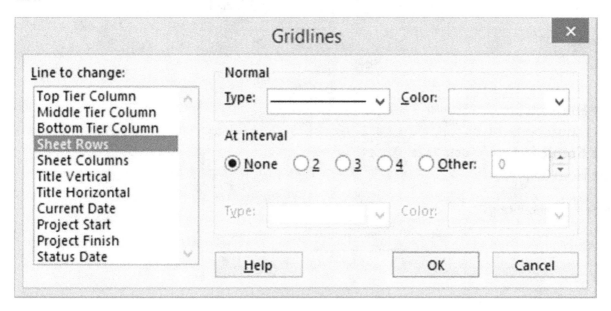

Step 7: Repeat to format additional lines.

Step 8: When you have finished getting all of the gridlines the way you want, select **OK**.

Changing Text Styles

To format the text on the Team Planner, use the following procedure.

Step 1: Select the **Team Planner Tools Format** tab from the Ribbon.

Step 2: Select **Text Styles**.

Step 3: In the *Text Styles* dialog box, select the following:

Step 3a: Choose the **Font** from the drop down list.

Step 3b: Select a **Font Style** from the list box.

Step 3c: Select the **Font Size** from the drop down list.

Step 3d: Check the **Underline** and/or **Strikethrough** boxes to apply these enhancements.

Step 3e: Select a **Color** from the drop down list.

Step 3f: Select a **Background Color** from the drop down list.

Text Styles

| Item to Change: | All | | OK |
| Font: | Font style: | Size: | Cancel |

@Adobe Fan Heiti Std
@Adobe Fangsong Std
@Adobe Gothic Std
@Adobe Heiti Std

Regular
Italic
Bold
Bold Italic

10
11
12
14

Underline Strikethrough

Color:

Sample

Background Color:

Background Pattern:

The Sample area shows a preview of your selections.

Step 1: Select **OK** to apply your Text Styles.

Changing Task Fill and Border Colors
To change fill and border colors, use the following procedure.

Step 1: Select the **Team Planner Tools Format** tab from the Ribbon.

Step 2: Select one of the following:

- Selected Tasks

- Auto Scheduled Tasks

- Manually Scheduled Tasks

- Actual Work

- External Tasks

- Late Tasks

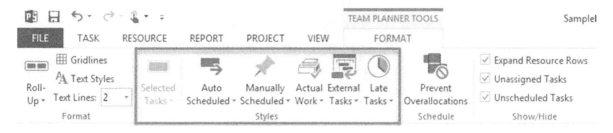

Step 3: Select **Fill Color** or **Border Color**.

Step 4: Select the color you want to use from the gallery.

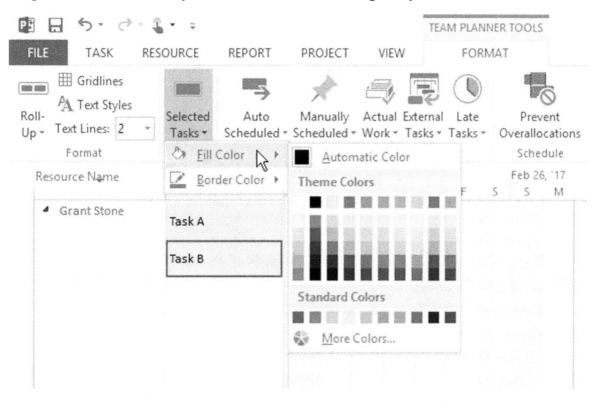

Practice applying different color combinations for different types of tasks and view the results.

Preventing Over Allocations

To prevent over allocations in the Team Planner view, use the following procedure.

Step 1: Select the **Team Planner Tools Format** tab from the Ribbon.

Step 2: Select **Prevent Over allocations**.

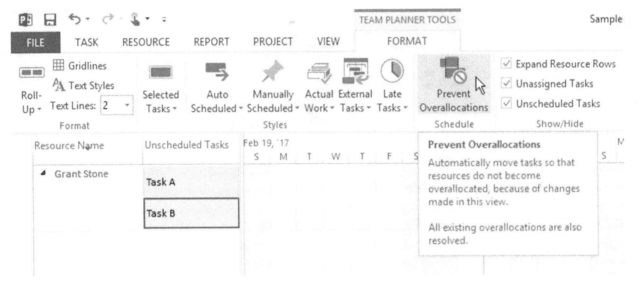

Practice moving tasks to see the results when over allocations might be created.

Showing and Hiding Information

To hide and show unassigned tasks and unscheduled tasks, use the following procedure.

Step 1: Select the **Team Planner Tools Format** tab from the Ribbon.

Step 2: Clear the **Unassigned Tasks** box to hide tasks that have not been assigned. Check the box to show them again.

Step 3: Clear the **Unscheduled Tasks** box to hide tasks that have not yet been scheduled. Check the box to show them again.

You can also choose whether to expand or condense Resource Rows.

Chapter 9 – Managing Risks and Measuring Performance

This chapter will help you further analyze the information that you have collected with your project schedule. First, you will learn how to review differences between planned, scheduled, and actual work. You will also learn how to find slack in the schedule so that you will know if tasks slip how it will affect the project schedule. This chapter also explains how to compare two versions of a project. Finally, we will look at calculating earned value analysis.

Reviewing Differences Between Planned, Scheduled, and Actual Work

To apply the work table to the Gantt chart, Task Usage, or Resource Usage views, use the following procedure.

Step 1: Select the **View** tab from the Ribbon.

Step 2: Select **Tables**.

Step 3: Select **Work**.

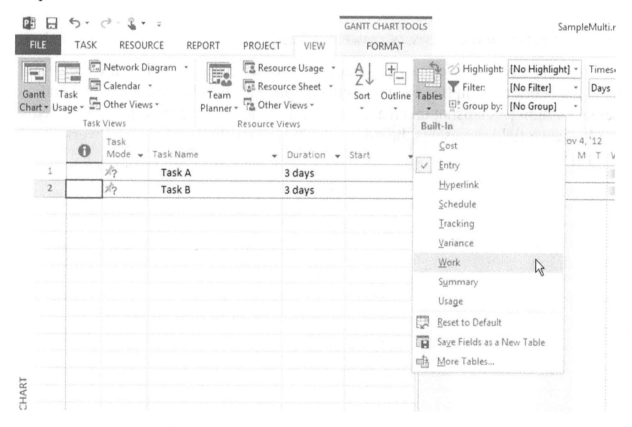

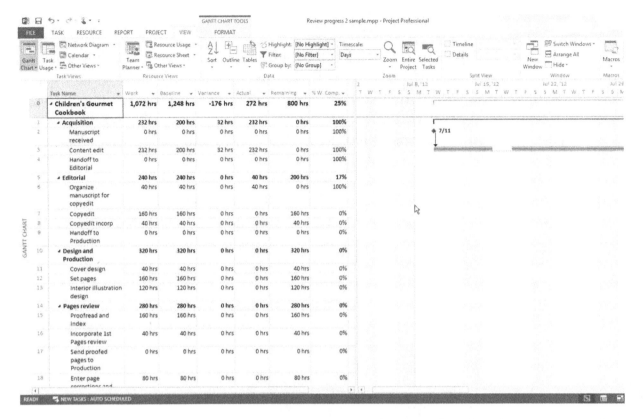

	Task Name	Work	Baseline	Variance	Actual	Remaining	% W. Comp.
0	⊿ Children's Gourmet Cookbook	1,072 hrs	1,248 hrs	-176 hrs	272 hrs	800 hrs	25%
1	⊿ Acquisition	232 hrs	200 hrs	32 hrs	232 hrs	0 hrs	100%
2	Manuscript received	0 hrs	0 hrs	0 hrs	0 hrs	0 hrs	100%
3	Content edit	232 hrs	200 hrs	32 hrs	232 hrs	0 hrs	100%
4	Handoff to Editorial	0 hrs	0 hrs	0 hrs	0 hrs	0 hrs	100%
5	⊿ Editorial	240 hrs	240 hrs	0 hrs	40 hrs	200 hrs	17%
6	Organize manuscript for copyedit	40 hrs	40 hrs	0 hrs	40 hrs	0 hrs	100%
7	Copyedit	160 hrs	160 hrs	0 hrs	0 hrs	160 hrs	0%
8	Copyedit incorp	40 hrs	40 hrs	0 hrs	0 hrs	40 hrs	0%
9	Handoff to Production	0 hrs	0 hrs	0 hrs	0 hrs	0 hrs	0%
10	⊿ Design and Production	320 hrs	320 hrs	0 hrs	0 hrs	320 hrs	0%
11	Cover design	40 hrs	40 hrs	0 hrs	0 hrs	40 hrs	0%
12	Set pages	160 hrs	160 hrs	0 hrs	0 hrs	160 hrs	0%
13	Interior illustration design	120 hrs	120 hrs	0 hrs	0 hrs	120 hrs	0%
14	⊿ Pages review	280 hrs	280 hrs	0 hrs	0 hrs	280 hrs	0%
15	Proofread and index	160 hrs	160 hrs	0 hrs	0 hrs	160 hrs	0%
16	Incorporate 1st Pages review	40 hrs	40 hrs	0 hrs	0 hrs	40 hrs	0%
17	Send proofed pages to Production	0 hrs	0 hrs	0 hrs	0 hrs	0 hrs	0%
18	Enter page corrections and	80 hrs	80 hrs	0 hrs	0 hrs	80 hrs	0%

Work and Actual columns have the same amount in completed tasks. Compare the amounts in the Work column (the total of Actual Work plus the Remaining Work) and the Baseline column (a snapshot taken at some point earlier in the project). For finished tasks, the Variance field represents the difference between actual and planned work.

The Task Usage sheet with the work table applied.

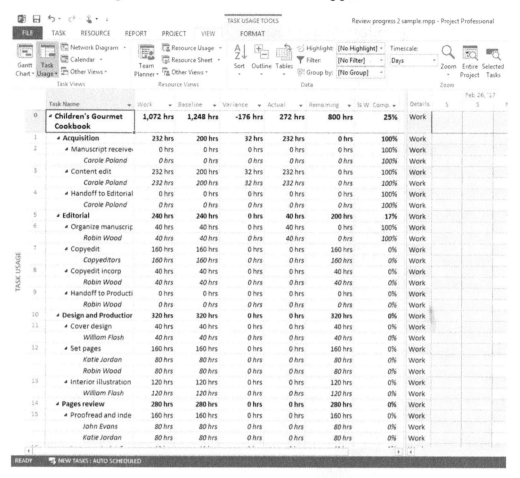

The Resource Usage table with the Work table applied.

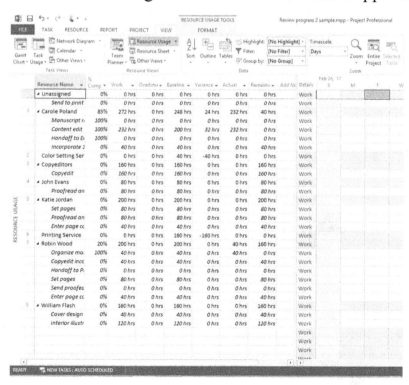

Finding Slack in the Schedule

To find slack in the schedule, use the following procedure.

Step 1: Select the **View** tab from the Ribbon.

Step 2: Select the arrow under **Gantt Chart**.

Step 3: Select **More Views**.

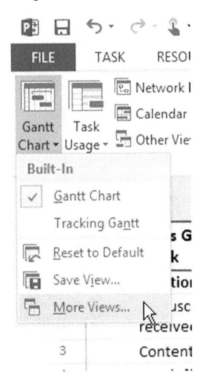

Step 4: In the *More Views* dialog box, select **Detail Gantt**. Select **Apply**.

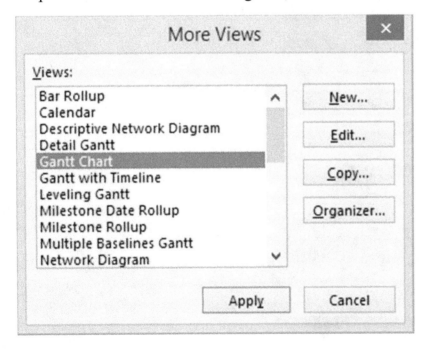

Step 5: Select **Tables** on the **View** tab.

Step 6: Select **Schedule**.

The slack is shown in the Free slack and Total Slack columns, as well as on the chart as thin bars to the right of tasks.

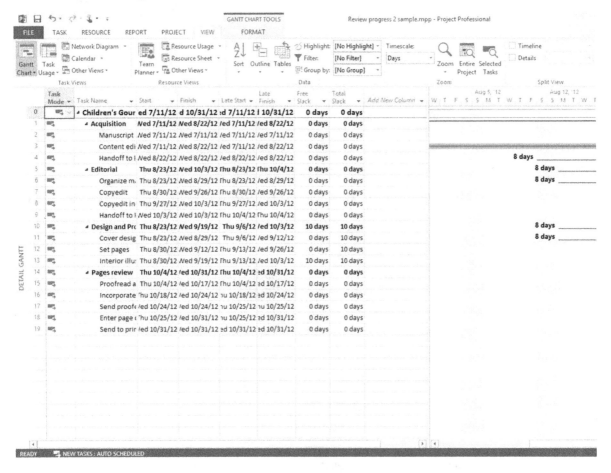

Comparing Two Versions of a Project

To compare projects, use the following procedure.

Step 1: Select the **Project** tab from the Ribbon.

Step 2: Select **Compare Projects**.

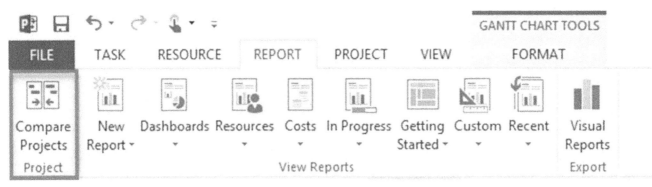

Step 3: In the *Compare Project Versions* dialog box, select the other project you want to use in the comparison from the drop down list (if it is open) or select **Browse** and navigate to the location of the other project.

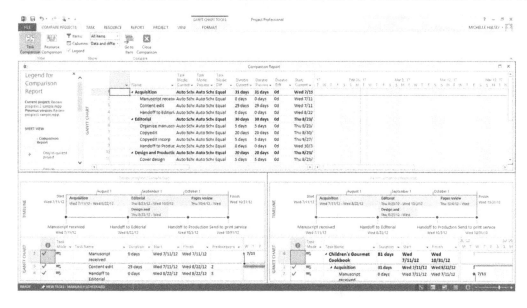

Step 4: Select the **Task Table** and **Resource Table** from the drop down lists to indicate the tables that have the data you want to compare. You can also select **None**.

Step 5: Select **OK**.

The Comparison opens. The Legend explains the color coding and indicators for the comparison report on the left side of the screen. The Comparison report contains only the differences between the two versions. It is not a consolidation of the two projects.

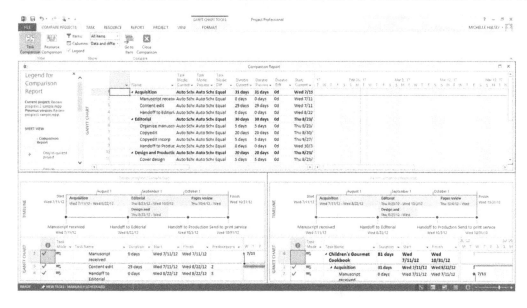

Calculating Earned Value Analysis

To set the type of earned value calculation, use the following procedure.

Step 1: Select the **File** tab to open the Backstage View.

Step 2: Select **Options**.

Step 3: Select **Advanced**.

Step 4: Scroll down to the **Earned Value** section.

Step 5: Select a calculation method from the **Default Task Earned Value Method** drop down list to indicate how Project calculates the budgeted cost of work scheduled (BCWS). BCWS is the baseline cost up to the status date that you choose. Budgeted cost values are stored in the baseline fields, or, if you saved multiple baselines, in the Baseline1 through Baseline10 fields. Note that changing this setting affects tasks added after the setting is changed.

Step 6: Select a **Baseline for Earned Value Calculations** from the drop down list.

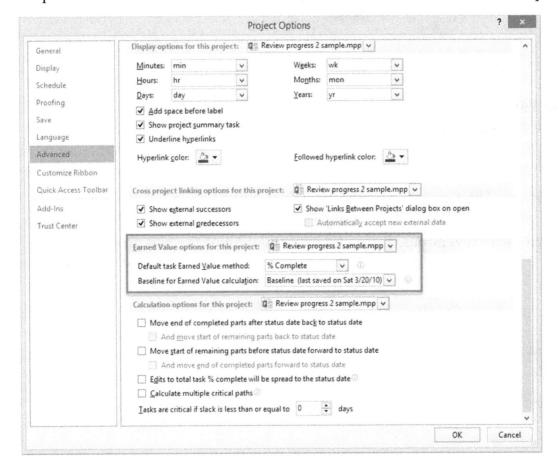

Step 7: Select **OK**.

Now we will view the calculations. To view the earned value analysis, use the following procedure.

Step 1: Select the **View** tab from the Ribbon.

Step 2: Select **Other Views**.

Step 3: In the *More Views* dialog box, select **Task Sheet**.

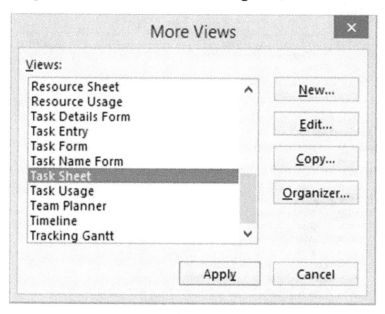

Step 4: Select **Apply**.

Step 5: Select **Tables** from the **View** tab.

Step 6: Select **More Tables**.

Step 7: From the *More Tables* dialog box, select **Earned Value, Earned Value Cost Indicators**, or **Earned Value Schedule Indicators**.

Step 8: Select **Apply**.

Hover your mouse over the column headings to see a description of each one.

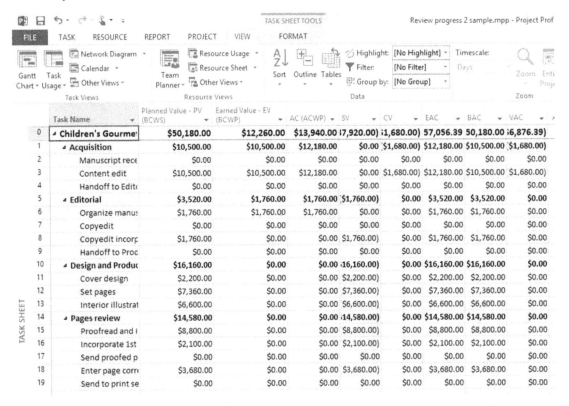

#	Task Name	Planned Value - PV (BCWS)	Earned Value - EV (BCWP)	AC (ACWP)	SV	CV	EAC	BAC	VAC
0	⊿ Children's Gourmet	$50,180.00	$12,260.00	$13,940.00	(7,920.00)	(1,680.00)	57,056.39	50,180.00	(6,876.39)
1	⊿ Acquisition	$10,500.00	$10,500.00	$12,180.00	$0.00	($1,680.00)	$12,180.00	$10,500.00	($1,680.00)
2	Manuscript rece	$0.00	$0.00	$0.00	$0.00	$0.00	$0.00	$0.00	$0.00
3	Content edit	$10,500.00	$10,500.00	$12,180.00	$0.00	($1,680.00)	$12,180.00	$10,500.00	($1,680.00)
4	Handoff to Edit	$0.00	$0.00	$0.00	$0.00	$0.00	$0.00	$0.00	$0.00
5	⊿ Editorial	$3,520.00	$1,760.00	$1,760.00	($1,760.00)	$0.00	$3,520.00	$3,520.00	$0.00
6	Organize manus	$1,760.00	$1,760.00	$1,760.00	$0.00	$0.00	$1,760.00	$1,760.00	$0.00
7	Copyedit	$0.00	$0.00	$0.00	$0.00	$0.00	$0.00	$0.00	$0.00
8	Copyedit incorp	$1,760.00	$0.00	$0.00	($1,760.00)	$0.00	$1,760.00	$1,760.00	$0.00
9	Handoff to Proc	$0.00	$0.00	$0.00	$0.00	$0.00	$0.00	$0.00	$0.00
10	⊿ Design and Produc	$16,160.00	$0.00	$0.00	(16,160.00)	$0.00	$16,160.00	$16,160.00	$0.00
11	Cover design	$2,200.00	$0.00	$0.00	$2,200.00)	$0.00	$2,200.00	$2,200.00	$0.00
12	Set pages	$7,360.00	$0.00	$0.00	$7,360.00)	$0.00	$7,360.00	$7,360.00	$0.00
13	Interior illustrat	$6,600.00	$0.00	$0.00	$6,600.00)	$0.00	$6,600.00	$6,600.00	$0.00
14	⊿ Pages review	$14,580.00	$0.00	$0.00	(14,580.00)	$0.00	$14,580.00	$14,580.00	$0.00
15	Proofread and i	$8,800.00	$0.00	$0.00	$8,800.00)	$0.00	$8,800.00	$8,800.00	$0.00
16	Incorporate 1st	$2,100.00	$0.00	$0.00	$2,100.00)	$0.00	$2,100.00	$2,100.00	$0.00
17	Send proofed p	$0.00	$0.00	$0.00	$0.00	$0.00	$0.00	$0.00	$0.00
18	Enter page corr	$3,680.00	$0.00	$0.00	$3,680.00)	$0.00	$3,680.00	$3,680.00	$0.00
19	Send to print se	$0.00	$0.00	$0.00	$0.00	$0.00	$0.00	$0.00	$0.00

You can also see a breakdown of the earned value of tasks by period, in order to determine the exact date that your project will run out of money.

Step 1: Select **Task Usage** from the **View** tab on the Ribbon.

Step 2: Select the **Format** tab from the Ribbon.

Step 3: Select **Add Details**.

Step 4: In the *Detail Styles* dialog box, select the Earned Value fields that you want to display. Select **Show**. Select **OK**.

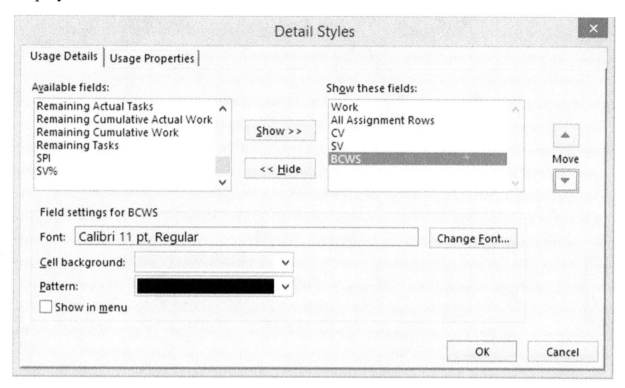

Chapter 10 – Communicating Project Information

Now that you are an expert at managing your project schedule, you will need to know how to communicate that information. This chapter explains some options for communicating Project information with those who do not have Project 2013. You will learn the specific procedures for copying a GIF image of your plan, publishing your project to a SharePoint list, attaching documents and including hyperlinks with your project. You will also learn how to print a view based on a specific date range.

About Sharing information

Project is not always enough, especially when many others who need to see the information do not have Project installed on their computers.

Project Web Access If your organization is using Microsoft Project Web App, you can ask the project manager to publish the project and then give you permission to view the project. Then you can view the project in Project Web App.

Copy Picture The person who created the project can use the Copy Picture feature to copy a .GIF image of the plan. The .GIF image can then be sent to you in e-mail, printed out, or added to a Web page.

Copy to another Office application Project 2013 contains enhanced functionality for basic copying and pasting project information while retaining formatting and column heading information. The person who created the project can copy the information from Project 2013 and paste it into applications like Word, Excel, PowerPoint, or Outlook. You can then view project information in those Office applications.

Visual reports The person who created the project can create a visual report that is designed for importing into and then viewing in either Excel or Visio.

SharePoint The person who created the report can save the report to a SharePoint site, without using Project Web App. You can then go to the SharePoint site to view and edit task and resource information associated with the Project. The project information that is edited on the SharePoint site will be copied back the original project automatically.

Copy the Timeline view The Timeline view in Project 2013 can be copied and pasted in an e-mail message or in any Office application for a quick view of Project progress along a graphic timeline.

Copying a .GIF Image of Your Plan

To copy of .GIF image of the project, use the following procedure.

Step 1: The screen should show the view and timescale that you want to copy. You may instead want to select the rows that you want to copy.

Step 2: Select the **Task** tab from the Ribbon.

Step 3: Select the arrow next to the **Copy** icon.

Step 4: Select **Copy Picture**.

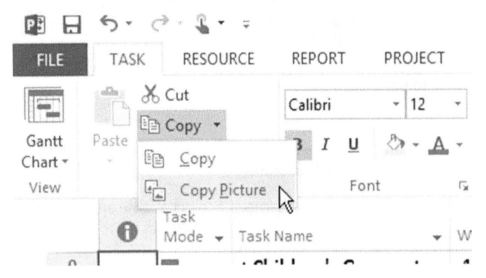

Step 5: In the *Copy Picture* dialog box, select **To GIF image file.** Select **Browse** to indicate the location where the file should be saved. You can change the file name, if desired.

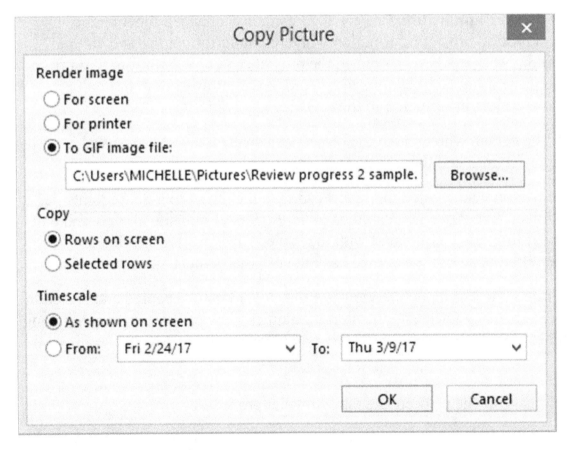

Step 6: Select whether to copy the **Rows on screen** or the **Selected rows**.

Step 7: Select whether to copy the timescale **As shown on screen** or for selected **dates** by indicating the start date and the end date to copy.

Step 8: Select **OK**.

With the GIF file, you can copy or insert it into another application like PowerPoint, Word, or an email message.

Publishing a Project to a SharePoint List

To publish a project to a SharePoint list, use the following procedure.

Step 1: Select the **File** tab to open the Backstage View.

Step 2: Select **Save & Send**.

Step 3: Select **Sync with Tasks Lists**.

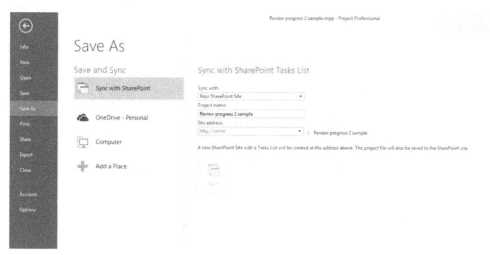

Step 1: In the **Site URL** drop down list, select the URL name of the SharePoint site. Do not select a URL with the name of the task list you want to use, just the site at this point.

Step 2: Select **Validate URL**.

Step 3: In the **Select an existing tasks list** drop down list, select the name of the SharePoint task list to which you want to sync. If you want to create a new list, enter the name.

Step 4: Select **Sync**.

Attaching Documents

To attach a document, use the following procedure.

Step 1: Double-click on the item to which you want to attach a document to open the Information dialog box for that item. In this example, we will use a resource.

Step 2: In the *Information* dialog box, select the **Notes** tab.

Step 3: Select the **Insert Object** icon.

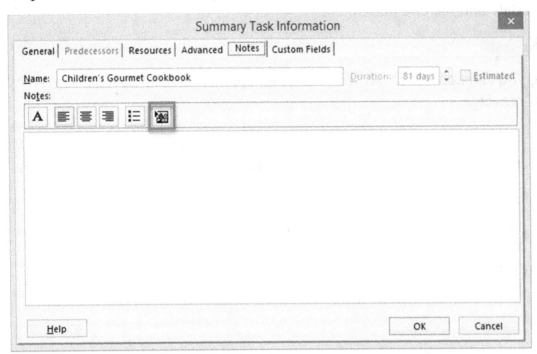

Step 4: In the *Insert Object* dialog box, select **Create from File**.

Step 5: Select **Browse** and navigate to the location of the file you want to use.

Step 6: To create a link so that if the document is updated, the information in Project is also updated, check the **Link** box.

Step 7: To display an icon for the document rather than the contents, check the **Display as Icon** box.

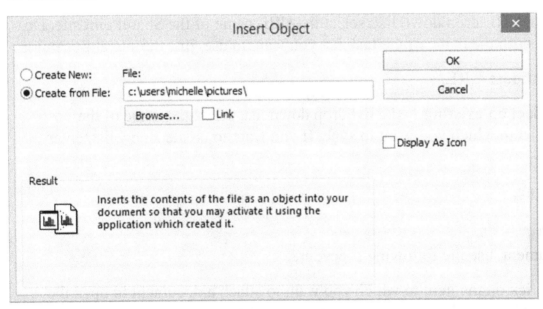

Step 8: Select **OK**.

Inserting Hyperlinks

To insert a hyperlink, use the following procedure.

Step 1: Select the task or other field in Project where you want to include a hyperlink.

Step 2: Right-click on the item.

Step 3: Select **Insert Hyperlink** from the context menu.

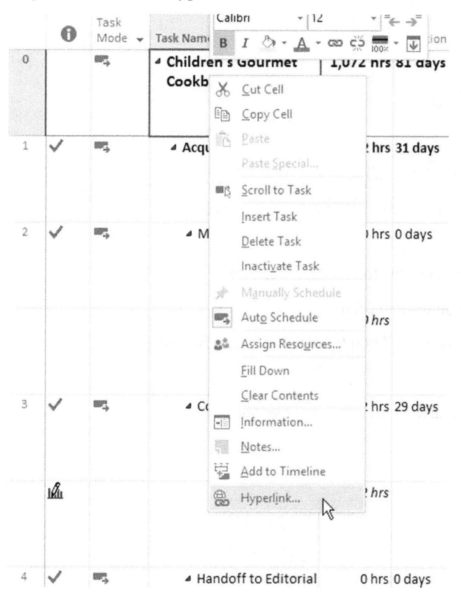

Step 4: In the *Insert Hyperlink* dialog box, use the **Look In** tools to find the location of the hyperlink destination. You can also enter or copy in the **Address**.

Step 5: Enter the **Text to display**.

Step 6: Select **OK**.

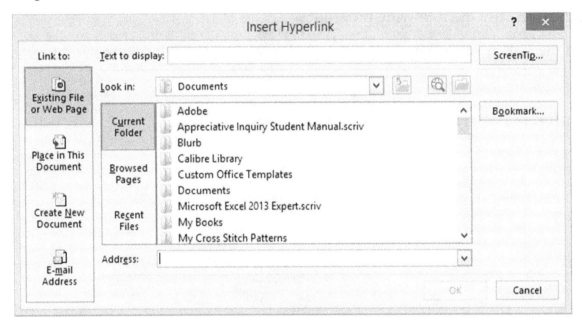

Step 7: Project displays the hyperlink icon in the Indicators column.

Printing Based on a Date Range

To print based on a date range, use the following procedure.

Step 1: Open the view that you want to print.

Step 2: Select the **File** tab from the Ribbon to open the Backstage view.

Step 3: Select **Print**.

Step 4: Use the Print Preview area to review your selection.

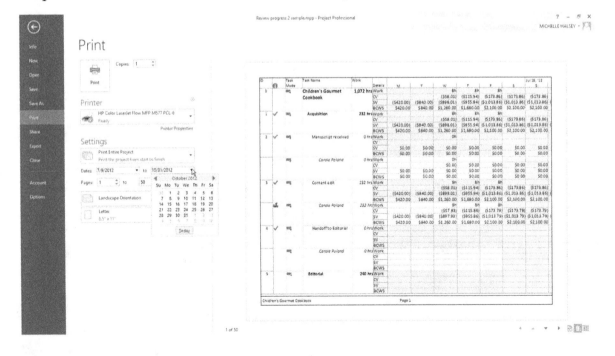

Step 5: In the **Dates** area, select the Start date and the End date that you want to print.

Step 6: Select **Print**.

Additional Titles

The Technical Skill Builder series of books covers a variety of technical application skills. For the availability of titles please see https://www.silvercitypublications.com/shop/. Note the Master Class volume contains the Essentials, Advanced, and Expert (when available) editions.

Current Titles

Microsoft Excel 2013 Essentials

Microsoft Excel 2013 Advanced

Microsoft Excel 2013 Expert

Microsoft Excel 2013 Master Class

Microsoft Word 2013 Essentials

Microsoft Word 2013 Advanced

Microsoft Word 2013 Expert

Microsoft Word 2013 Master Class

Microsoft Project 2013 Essentials

Microsoft Project 2013 Advanced

Microsoft Project 2013 Expert

Microsoft Project 2013 Master Class

Microsoft Visio 2010 Essentials

Microsoft Visio 2010 Advanced

Microsoft Visio 2010 Master Class

Coming Soon

Microsoft Access 2013 Essentials

Microsoft Access 2013 Advanced

Microsoft Access 2013 Expert

Microsoft Access 2013 Master Class

Microsoft PowerPoint 2013 Essentials

Microsoft PowerPoint 2013 Advanced

Microsoft PowerPoint 2013 Expert

Microsoft PowerPoint 2013 Master Class

Microsoft Outlook 2013 Essentials

Microsoft Outlook 2013 Advanced

Microsoft Outlook 2013 Expert

Microsoft Outlook 2013 Master Class

Microsoft Publisher 2013 Essentials

Microsoft Publisher 2013 Advanced

Microsoft Publisher 2013 Master Class

Windows 7 Essentials

Windows 8 Essentials